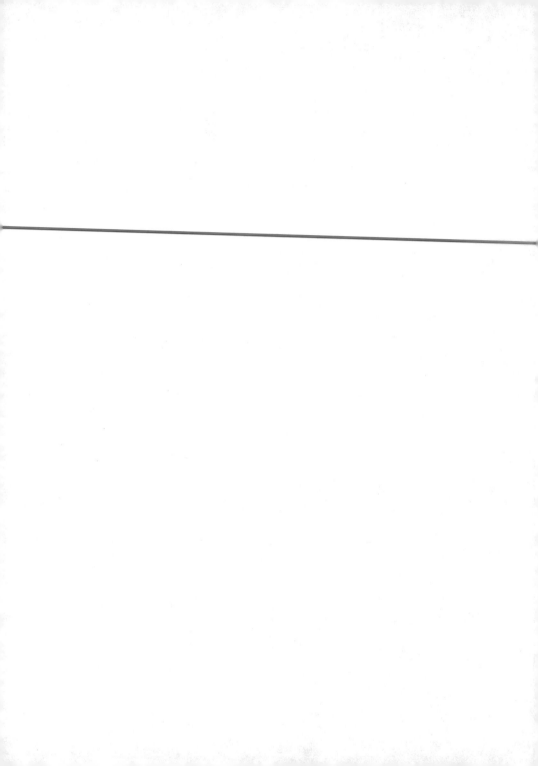

A Future of Ice

Poems and Stories of a Japanese Buddhist

MIYAZAWA KENJI

Translated and with an Introduction
by Hiroaki Sato

NORTH POINT PRESS
San Francisco 1989

The translator wishes to dedicate this book to
Lindley Williams Hubbell Sensei

Cover illustration by Gen Yamaguchi,
Human Beings, 1953. Color woodcut, numbered 47/50,
462 × 375 mm.
Achenbach Foundation for Graphic Arts purchase,
1965.68.117. Reproduced by permission of The Fine
Arts Museums of San Francisco.

LIBRARY OF CONGRESS
CATALOGING-IN-PUBLICATION DATA
Miyazawa, Kenji, 1896–1933.
   A future of ice.
   Half-title: Poems and stories of a Japanese Bud-
   dhist.
   Enl. ed. of: Spring & asura. 1973.
   1. Miyazawa, Kenji, 1896–1933—Translations, En-
   glish. I. Sato, Hiroaki, 1942–   . II. Miyazawa,
   Kenji, 1896–1933. Haru to shura. English. III. Ti-
   tle. IV. Title: Poems and stories of a Japanese Bud-
   dhist.
PL833.I95A25 1989   895.6'14   88-33027
ISBN 0-86547-373-0 (pbk.)

North Point Press
850 Talbot Avenue
Berkeley, California
94706

Contents

THREE STORIES

Acknowledgments

This is a revised, greatly expanded edition of *Spring & Asura: Poems of Kenji Miyazawa* (Chicago Review Press, 1973). Several translations in that book were later revised, and some other poems translated, for the anthology *From the Country of Eight Islands* (Doubleday and the University of Washington Press, 1981; reissued by Columbia University Press, 1986). Some of the tanka and other poems not in the original edition appeared in *Montemora* and *Telephone*.

The Introduction first appeared, in a substantially different form, in the December 26, 1983, edition of the *Mainichi Daily News*, under the title "I Am Asura Incarnate."

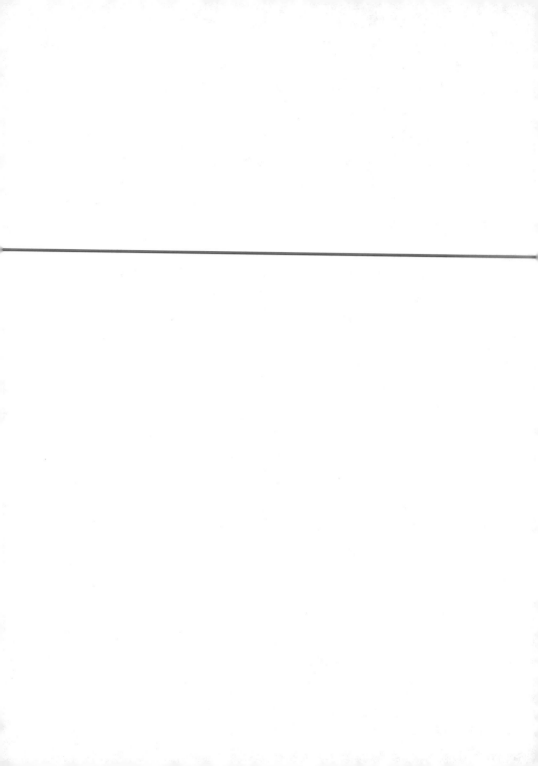

Introduction

Miyazawa Kenji (1896–1933)—here his and other Japanese names are given the Japanese way, family name first—is probably the only modern Japanese poet who is deified. A good part of the deification may come from a piece called "November 3rd." Opening with the phrases "neither yielding to rain / nor yielding to wind / yielding neither to / snow nor to summer heat," it describes in simple, moving words the poet's wishes to do good for others while remaining humble and obscure himself.

"November 3rd" was found posthumously in a pocket notebook Miyazawa is thought to have used beginning in late 1931, two years before his death. Though the text is broken into lines, considering his approach to versification at the time, it is likely to have been meant more as a prayer than a poem. (The translation in this volume attempts to reproduce the original format.) Yet as early as 1942, the Japanese government, then in the early stage of the Pacific War, used it as a propaganda piece, apparently deciding that it would help inculcate the sacrificial spirit in the general populace. A few years later Tanikawa Tetsuzō, a well-known philosopher and the father of the poet Tanikawa Shuntarō (born 1931), called it the "noblest" Japanese poem of modern times, while describing the poet as the only man of letters before whose grave he would want to genuflect. Since then, "November 3rd" has not only been used in school textbooks, but printed on an assortment of souvenir products.

The deification of Miyazawa may also derive from the way he lived. The aggressive promotion of the man as a saint by his surviving family members and others confounds much of his belief and action. But there seems little doubt that Miyazawa, a devout Buddhist of an activist sect, was profoundly concerned about the plight of the peasants of his region, Iwate, which was known as the "Tibet of Japan" for its unaccommodating climate, topography, and soil, and for its frequent crop failures. After studying and teaching at two agricultural schools, Miyazawa put his knowledge to practical use. And for the few years after he began helping the peasants learn modern, scientific farming methods, he forced himself, unscientifically, to subsist on a poorer diet than even the local people were accustomed to, and ruined his health. One thing that makes this story ennobling, if you will, is the fact that as the first son of a well-to-do businessman, albeit a pawnbroker of used clothes, Miyazawa did not have to do any such thing. Furthermore, for religious reasons he led an ascetic life and remained unmarried.

Should, however, "November 3rd" and a bare biographical sketch, such as I have just given, create an image of Miyazawa as the sort of pious wimp you would want to avoid, that would be most unfortunate. Miyazawa was no weak-kneed murmurer of ineffectual pieties. He compared himself to an *asura*, in Buddhist belief the contentious, sometimes malevolent giant who ranks between the human and the beast, a sort of perpetually dissatisfied trouble-maker. In *"Haru to Shura"* (Spring & Asura), the title poem of his first book of poetry, published in 1924 at his own expense, he put it this way:

> At the bottom of the light in April's atmospheric strata,
> spitting, gnashing, pacing back and forth,
> I am Asura incarnate. . . .

Miyazawa thought this image of himself as an *asura* important enough to use the title *Spring & Asura* for three unpublished collections of his poems. And the picture of Miyazawa that emerges from his poems is that of a man who is entranced by the things that happen around him, and eternally restless.

He frequently took long walks, day and night, furiously scribbling in his notebook with a pencil hung from his neck on a string. As a result, a great many lines of his poetry and, indeed, a good many of his poems are detailed descriptions of things observed. So, for example, "Koiwai Farm," a poem of more than eight hundred lines, is largely a catalogue of what he saw as he walked one day from a railway station to a Western-style farm established by three entrepreneurs in 1891.

His fascination with what was happening around him and his delight in describing observed things rarely produced trivial or merely curious pieces. He was, for one thing, blessed with a singular, almost hallucinatory imagination. As the critic Yoshimoto Ryūmei has noted, Miyazawa's writings are so attractive because of "the extraordinarily free placement of the eyes." In one moment, the scope is as sweeping and grand as if seen by "the eyes attached to a body giant enough to reach the top of an exceptionally tall building"; in the next instant, it is as microscopically detailed as if seen by "the eyes attached to the head of a crawling, minute insect."

Miyazawa also had a highly developed sense of drama and humor, as exemplified by such dramatic monologues as "The Prefectural Engineer's Statement Regarding Clouds." These qualities, when blended with Buddhist pantheism and a belief in science that was tempered by a fine sensibility, created a unique poetic world that is at once intense and light, joyful and moving. It is a world yet to be matched by another Japanese poet, ancient or modern.

As might be expected, Miyazawa in real life was often frustrated in trying to carry out his good intentions among the peasants. This may be discerned from ruefully comic poems, such as "Hateful Kuma Eats His Lunch," and other more straightforward pieces. Many peasants no doubt valued his new agricultural knowledge. But many also regarded him as an obnoxious do-gooder who intruded into their centuries-old ways of doing things. Though he himself didn't say so explicitly, it is thought that he was beset with a sense of failure toward the end of his life. Some say that what appear to be, at least on the surface, innocuous pieties in "November 3rd" in fact hide Miyazawa's admission of defeat—although others say that those "pieties" are the ultimate expression of Buddhist sincerity as Miyazawa understood it.

Still, Miyazawa maintained a resilient soul. An outstanding manifestation of this is the poem "Pictures of the Floating World," whose sensuality may seem so uncharacteristic of this determinedly ascetic poet. He wrote it after seeing a wood-block print exhibition in Tokyo in 1928. Indeed, he had a lifelong interest in this genre of art. Once he wrote an essay on the technical aspects of print-making. Another time, in 1931, he composed advertisement copy for prints to help a friend start a new business.

Miyazawa began writing poems in the traditional 5-7-5-7-7-syllable *tanka* form at age fifteen, in 1911. He continued to write mainly in this form until 1920, when he put together a "tanka manuscript" of 735 pieces. In preparing it he recast, for some unstated reasons, what were originally poems written in the standard single-line format into poems of one to six lines.

Such lineation of the tanka, normally regarded as a "one-line poem," began with the publication, in 1910, of NAKIWARAI (Crying, Laughing) by Toki Aika (1885–1980), who broke up every piece in the book into three lines. The practice was followed by some notable poets, among them Ishikawa Takuboku (1886–1912), who would become the best-known writer of three-line tanka. Miyazawa's lineation was much freer and might have influenced the later development of this poetic form had the manuscript been published. However, even though many of the pieces had appeared in school magazines and other places, he strictly proscribed the publication of the manuscript. This he did probably with the thought, at least initially, of revising the pieces, as he evidently continued to do for a few years. Then, perhaps, other things began to preoccupy him. In any event, the two poems he wrote several hours before his death are also in the tanka form. A fair selection of tanka, including those two "last poems," is translated here.

Not long after putting together the tanka manuscript Miyazawa switched to free verse. In between, he wrote a group of poems called "Winter Sketches," which are regarded as transitional pieces.

Free verse became the accepted standard in Japanese poetry during the 1910s with the appearance of such books as *Dōtei* (Journey) by Takamura

Kōtarō (1883–1956), published in 1914, and *Tsuki ni Hoeru* (Howling at the Moon) by Hagiwara Sakutarō (1886–1942), published in 1917. Miyazawa continued to write in this format to the end of his life, although in 1928 he also began writing *bungo-shi*, which employed syllabic patterns and literary rather than colloquial language. The reasons for his reversion, if it was such, are obscure, and of the 262 *bungo-shi* he composed, only a handful rival his free verse in strength and intensity. Toward the end of his life he also wrote some haiku and even a few sequences of *renga*, linked verse. But these, too, are not remarkable. All the non-tanka poems translated here have been selected from his free verse.

In addition to poetry, Miyazawa wrote a good many short stories, mostly for children. The best of these stories, written from 1918 to the year of his death, are characterized by the same qualities that make his poetry stand out: keen power of observation, imagination, Buddhist vision, and a sense of humor. Many are stark, at times brutal. And even when compassion is the theme, the resolution of the conflict is usually realistic and credible. Here I have translated only three of the stories, a very small sampling of the many-faceted world Miyazawa constructed.

During his lifetime Miyazawa remained a largely obscure local writer. Now he is recognized as one of the three or four greatest poets, and surely the most imaginative spinner of children's stories, of twentieth-century Japan. It is my hope that these translations will show him to be worthy of that recognition.

I thank Michael O'Brien, Robert Fagan, and Nancy Rossiter for reading and helping improve all the translations. Kyoko Selden and Eliot Weinberger did the same with "Koiwai Farm." For all their generous help, whatever errors and infelicities remain are all my own.

Hiroaki Sato
New York City, 1988

A Future of Ice

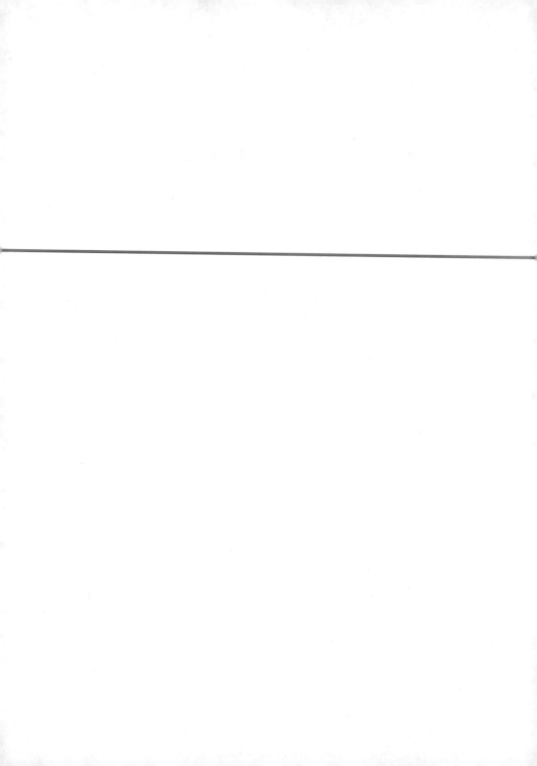

POEMS

Early Poems in Tanka Form

APRIL 1909

Father father why in front of the superintendent did you wind your large
silver watch?

JANUARY 1911

Holding a gun
against his chest
and fumblingly
eating
cookies—
that must be Yoshino.

———

Making a syrupy sweet fire at midnight
in a mountain valley I sing alone.

———

Built in a small upriver vale:
a small school,
a small shrine.

APRIL 1912

The white sky has pressed on me
as if to pull my hair strand by strand.

———

Like the craze on porcelain, fine branches
apportion the lonely white sky.

———

When all the shrubs
have darkened like hair
a yellow dog is there
tumbling in the snow.

———

In the depth of its brown eyes
hiding something evil a bull looks at me.

APRIL 1914

When the thermometer's
blue-gleaming mercury
boundlessly went on rising
I closed my eyes, I did.

———

As I go aflutter
through the morning corridor

my eyes hurt
at the green of trees and the light of sky.

———

I alone
can't sleep can't sleep;
hung in the midnight window
moon scorched clay.

———

Truly like those parrots breathing inaudibly
all the nurses are fast asleep.

———

A bloodshot
bow-taut moon
comes in my window
midnight and warps its mouth.

———

Even birds
don't cry now;
that bloodshot
one-eye may have left the sky.

———

You, wholesome
beautiful one,
I'm utterly ill,
aren't my eyes yellow, fox-like?

7

Tattered,
red, my throat—
sadly
with father who's ill again
I find myself quarreling.

———

Tray of blood
with leeches swimming in it—
in this house
evening sun's yellow
evening sun's yellow.

———

Buttercup pearlwort flowers and through their clusters a single rusted
water line.

———

Again, alone
I come to the woods, mimic dove calls,
and dig sad, small
lily bulbs.

———

Head heavy,
noon lonesome,
I have cut open
a rusty fish eyeball.

―――――

On the farther bank
people   stack stones
people   stack
stones but lonesome:
the mercury river.

―――――

In the east purple-gold Bhechadjaguru
because of the sickly sky has graciously appeared.

―――――

Because the flames
in which I live are blue,
busily
flashing, burning,
winter seems to have come.

―――――

I long for you
this cloud-dark day:
one after another
Clown-Festival carts pass.

―――――

The wheat at Shiwa Castle must have ripened;
its yellow is
bright on this side
of the sky where you live.

———

Loneliness is
the wallpaper's white,
the river flowing   gleaming wallpaper-white.

———

The night rain
half-damaged
my lily;
as dew sparkles on it
a mosquito comes, trembles.

———

In the autumn wind
deep in my head a tiny bone
must have splintered:
there was that sound.

———

Kinky
shadow-colored clouds:
and now in winter
the teacher's dead, crows fly.

APRIL 1915

A snatch of cloud
reflected on the wings

of a beetle nibbling parsley flowers
flies in the valley sky.

MARCH 1916

Right next to a mountain
with a frowning face,
isolated,
white sun floats up, stays

_____

Out of the navy blue of a mountain below the clouds comes a faint smell of
iodine trembling.

JULY 1916

Frost-cloudy:
toward this harvested field where crickets cry
comes a horse carrying
black manure.

_____

Far-off
mountains etched at back,
as if in a dream geese have appeared.

_____

The director of the school's postal service
(emptiness of cherries)
has died young.

———

Through the windowpane
comes this sunlight
sunlight   desk
someone's turf.

———

End-of-month moon,
its black eyelids well exposed,
hangs in the sky
which is turning white white.

———

"What can I do for you?"
"Sake sales-slip."
"Who are you? Your name?"
"Takahashi Mogizu."
"All right. Wait a minute."

———

Yellow leaves fallen,
ivory-carved white birches
are crowned with the midday moon.

———

Feeling as if riding the Siberian train
in a clear morning, in a classroom
I'm ill.

———

The Toné River quietly slides, entering the white daybreak cirri in the
Plain of Heaven.

Cypress Song

First Day, Daytime

By chance
I look at the window:
a single cypress is being disturbed,
utterly terrifying.

A storm comes,
sky pale-white—
casually disturbed, bending,
a single cypress.

Because in the frequent winds
the cypress bends, disturbed,
the square window looks different.

(A bright cloud reeling rushing in the blue void, elongated,
shaking, that's winter's voice.)

Second Day, Night

As snow falls,
the bad cypress of yesterday noon
stands erect in the form of a bodhisattva.

Bad cypress,
disturbed by day, the bad cypress
covered with snow
assumes the form of a bodhisattva.

Third Day, Evening

In twilight,
standing straight, that cypress,
at the back of that cypress, silver gray clouds.

Windowpanes
if they fall, will make a square void;
in that void
a twilight cypress.

Fourth Day, Night

Black cypress
sneaking up to a slice of cloud where moonlight pools,
what are you plotting?

White cloud, night's white cloud,
the moonlight is heavy,
beware of that bad cypress.

Fifth Day, Night

Snow drops, the cypress sways;
steely sky
rising fragrant, the moon, playful.

Vaguely
in the gas of moonlight
the cypress shakes snow off its branches.
> (This boundless world has nothing, not even a poppy seed,
> for which a bodhisattva won't forsake himself.)

The moonlight,
cool, pale, about three o'clock,
the cypress swishes the snow off its branches.

Sixth Day, Daytime

Young in age
the cypress sways, and the day sings;
from the azure sky fall cotton snowflakes.

Sixth Day, Evening

Sunflowers'
wilted stalks, how many of them,
encircle the darkening cypress.

Seventh Day, Night

In the twilight
snow the black cypress stands,
its center slightly tilting against the sky.
> (Cypress, cypress, are you truly a living thing?
> You seem deeply related to me.
> How often have we met since the old days?
> Cypress, you don't recognize me.)

X-th Day

For a while
resigned to the continuing exams
I saw the cypress waver in the westering sun.

The faintly blue
sky, hushed,
ether bullet traces are about to burst
as the winter ends.

APRIL 1917

What trembles
in the ultramarine sky:
fragrance
of tree flowers and a black bee's drone.

_____

Seven Forests
splashed with white clouds
spread
like a jesting beast's fur.

MAY 1917

The burnt scar of Mt. Takahora
where evening sun pours—
someone privately
snickers at it.

_____

Ceasing to respond
to my whistles
a bird has now
entered trees fluttering their leaves.

_____

Out of the crack between folded twilight clouds peers a slice of heaven.

As I move away from the Bunsen burner
near dusk
pearlwort flowers
the color of the moon.

———

Kashiwa Field
the Galaxy crosses white and white—
I went there with a fire
but horses didn't come running.

———

(Sliding through the field where lilies-of-the-valley glisten
the toes of the wind
weep and laugh.)

———

Arms spread,
chasing a horse in a suspicious manner—
a naked man
in a field of lilies-of-the-valley.

———

Suddenly dropping a half-eaten
cherry
a bird has detached itself from a nutmeg branch.

JULY 1917

Riverside
midday-wavering stone wall—
as I enter drowsiness
a bird again cries.

—————

The amber sky
frozen above
a sea of clouds—
giant skinks
in herds are crossing it.

—————

As I walk thinking of a hairpin with a tuft dangling from it, the night sky's
                                        so deep a blast furnace burns.

—————

At daybreak
in the mists on a pass meagerly
flows a smell of blue tomatoes.

—————

Fully
loaded with pollen a small bee with blue eyes
circles my four lilies.

———

Because sparklingly
the rain has left and not a soul's around
a goose rushed at me and bit my leg.

———

Through the cracked
frozen yellow rose dawn sky
breathlessly   a bird dashes.

———

Through the night
the horse came carrying sulfur—now
in the morning sun he's deep
in thought.

MAY 1918

In the not-darkening   citrine sky
blue and desolate   trees stand
rain   falling straight.

———

And now
it has become a twilight sky,
far beyond the blue trees
a crow flying.

———

Right below a nickel cloud, irritated,
there's an arc lamp burning white white.

———

Though one after another
silver clouds cut across the window
the envy lies blue, stagnant in the room.

Andersen: Swan Song

"Listen" („*Höre*,")
again
the moon has spoken;
gently
Andersen's moon has spoken.

———

From the sky
tiny cold whorls descending,
at the top of a paulownia
a crow trembles.

———

To the modest
branches of a spring walnut
golden babies
have come to hang.

■◻ Lamenting Dr. Ishimaru's Death

Casually pressing his pain he used to stand—
the way he looked then   is what I think of.

———

Sea swallows
congregate, circle
at daybreak
catching blue fish   while clouds droop and fall.

From "Winter Sketches"

About the time white light fills the room
outside the starch-painted window
someone's stretching on his toes again and again,
someone's jumping up again and again.
That sure is Sonnental.

―――

These pine trees on this street
are, may I say, too crowded.
Their branches are too crowded—
the nice snow on those ridges
and, look, the copper powder on that mountain surface
you can't see anything, nothing at all, can you? How about thinning them
a bit?

―――

On that stubby rock cliff a while ago
the thing that started falling wasn't rain, I tell you.
Looked like sleet. Was sleet, I tell you.

―――

What presses close is the feel of a grassfield.
The Pleiades give a white yawn.
From a marker two cedars rise,
faintly extending to the Pleiades.

―――――

Because of the thawing flood   the cedars
were all covered with mud.
And from then on the sky was white,
the snow lay yellow,
the hawk flew, mouth open, in the sky,
and the crow cried, bending its body.

―――――

There's something that presses my eardrums from somewhere.
The voice that's rustling, singing, in the direction of the black woods—
I can't clearly tell what it is.

―――――

I looked back at the tracks I'd come along. There it was gray and surely   it
had turned into a field of death. The same was true of the darkness and of
the withered grass.

―――――

(What can you see
if you look beyond
the sandy field of cacti of Mexico?)
(We can see the volcano of Popocatepetl.)
(That's right. Well then what can you see if you look downward from the
volcano of Popocatepetl?)
(If we look downward from the top of Mt. Popocatepetl we can mainly see
cacti and things.)

When I put on my coat
and went out of my house
only Canis Major
was shining out of
black clouds torn to pieces.

My temples felt a sudden chill,
so, thinking it was hail I hurriedly looked up at the sky;
only above my head the cloud had a hole,
and lonesome stars were shining fully in it.

Then again I wrote that down
and wondering which constellation, looked up there once more;
this time it was already full of vague clouds
and in the distance a train rushed with a roar.

Truly I'd like to weep.
What on earth I'm sorrowing about
I can't tell, and that's what gives me pain.
A black cloud tears apart and hides the stars.
I tread the mud road.

Small roadside bush,
I'll give you my body.
The row of lights at the station wavers,
and the atmospheric strata also seem weeping.

■□ Proem

The phenomenon called "I"
is a blue illumination
of the hypothesized, organic alternating current lamp
    (a compound of all transparent ghosts)
a blue illumination
of the karmic alternating current lamp
which flickers busily, busily
with landscapes, with everyone
yet remains lit with such assuredness
    (the light persists, the lamp lost).

In the twenty-two months, which I perceive
lie in the direction of the past
I have linked these pieces on paper with mineral ink
    (they flicker with me,
      everyone feels them simultaneously)
each a chain of shadow and light,
mental sketches as they are,
which have been kept until now.

About these, the man, the galaxy, Asura, or the sea urchin,
eating cosmic dust, breathing air or salt water,
may each think up a fresh ontology,

but any one of them too will be no more than a scene in the mind.
Yet certainly these landscapes recorded here
are as they are recorded;
if they represent nothing, that's the way nothing is;
to some degree this holds true of everyone
        (because just as everything is everyone in me,
        so I am everything in everyone).

But while these words, supposed to have been copied correctly
in the accumulation of the vast bright times
of the Cenozoic era and alluvial epoch,
already change their structures and contents
in the light and shadow that's equal to a dot
        (or in Asura's billion years)
the tendency could be there
that both the printer and I
perceive them as unchangeable.
Because, just as we perceive our senses,
landscapes, and personalities,
just as we all merely perceive them,
so the records and histories, or the history of the earth,
together with their various data
(under the temporal, spatial restrictions of karma),
are no more than what we perceive.
Perhaps, two thousand years from now,
an appropriately different geology may win the time,
apposite evidence may turn up successively from the past,
everyone may think that two thousand years ago
colorless peacocks filled the blue sky,
fresh bachelors of arts may excavate

wonderful fossils somewhere from the glittering frozen nitrogen
at the top stratum of the atmosphere,
or discover in a stratification plane
of Cretaceous sandstone
the enormous footprints of an invisible mankind.

All these propositions are asserted
in the four-dimensional extension
as the attributes of imagination and time.

20 January 1924

■□ Refractive Index

When a closer one of the Seven Forests
is far brighter than it is in the water
and extremely large
why do I have to tread on a bumpy frozen road,
tread on this bumpy snow,
and hurry myself
like a gloomy letter-carrier
      (again Aladdin takes the lamp)
toward the kinky zinc clouds beyond?

6 January 1922

The Snow on Saddle Mountain

The only thing you can count on
is the snow on the string of Saddle Mountain peaks.
The fields and the woods
look either frowzy or dulled
and you can't count on them at all,
so, although it's really such a yeasty,
opaque blizzard,
the only thing that sends faint hope
is Saddle Mountain
      (this is one old-fashioned religion)

6 January 1922

The Thief

Under the pale blue constellation, the Skeleton, toward daybreak,
he crosses the irregular reflections in the frozen mud
and steals the one celadon jar
placed outside the store.
Abruptly he stops his long, dark legs,
puts his hands to his ears,
and listens to the music box, the electric poles.

2 March 1922

■◻ Love & Fever

Today my forehead dark,
I can't even look straight at the crows.
    My sister, just about now
    in a cold gloomy bronze-hued ward,
      begins to be burnt by transparent rosy fire.
Truly, though, sister,
today I too feel weighed down, terrible,
so I won't pick up willow flowers and come.

20 March 1922

Spring & Asura

Out of the gray steel of imagination
akebi vines entwine the spider web,
wildrose bush, humus marsh
everywhere, everywhere, such designs of arrogance
  (when more busily than noon woodwind music
  amber fragments pour down)
how bitter, how blue is the anger!
At the bottom of the light in April's atmospheric strata,
spitting, gnashing, pacing back and forth,
I am Asura incarnate
(the landscape sways in my tears)
Shattered clouds to the limit of visibility
   in heaven's sea of splendor
     sacred crystalline winds sweep
       spring's row of *Zypressen*
        absorbs ether, black,
         at its dark feet
           the snow ridge of T'ien-shan glitters
             (waves of heat haze & white polarization)
           yet the True Words are lost
         the clouds, torn, fly through the sky.
    Ah, at the bottom of the brilliant April,
   gnashing, burning, going back and forth,
I am Asura incarnate
  (chalcedonous clouds flow,
  where does he sing, that spring bird?)
The sun shimmers blue,

Asura and forest, one music,
　　and from heaven's bowl that caves in and dazzles,
　　　throngs of clouds like calamites extend,
　　　　branches sadly proliferating
　　　all landscapes twofold
　　treetops faint, and from them
　a crow flashes up
　　(when the atmospheric strata become clearer
　　　& cypresses, hushed, rise in heaven)
Someone coming through the gold of grassland,
someone casually assuming a human form,
in rags & looking at me, a farmer,
does he really see me?
At the bottom of the sea of blinding atmospheric strata
(the sorrow blue blue and deep)
Zypressen sway gently,
the bird severs the blue sky again
　(the True Words are not here,
　Asura's tears fall on the earth)

As I breathe the sky anew
lungs contract faintly white
(body, scatter in the dust of the sky)
The top of a ginkgo tree glitters again
the *Zypressen* darker
sparks of the clouds pour down.

8 April 1922

■□ Springday Curse

What the hell has come over you?
Do you know what this means?
Hair dark and long,
she closes her mouth, hushed,
that's all there is to it.
>   Spring goes silly over grass ears,
>   all your guesses will fade
>   (Here it's all grassblue, dark
>   and terribly empty)
Cheeks slightly red, eyes brown,
that's all there is to it.
>   (This bitter blue cold
>   This bitter blue cold)

10 April 1922

Daybreak

The rolling snow
gets bright peach juice poured into it,
the moon left unmelted in the blue sky
purring gently to heaven
drinks once again the diffused light
   (*pāra-samgate bodhi svāhā*)

10 April 1922

Sunlight and Withered Grass

From somewhere a chisel stabs
and a blue haze of light paraffin;
circling, circling, a crow;
crow's creak . . . crow tool
(Will this change)
(It will)
(Will this change)
(It will)
(How about this)
(It won't)
(If that's the case, hey, bring here
a bundle of clouds, quick)
(Yes, it will change, it will)

23 April 1922

A Letter

The rain falls negligently,
a transparent, intermittent rain that falls through flickering imagination.
What gets wet are horsetail and wood sorrel.
The hair of the cypress has grown too long.

My chest cavity is dark and hot
I think it has already begun to ferment.

This side of the green wet bank
a rubberized poncho the color of blue mud
trudges slowly, slowly—
it's such a painful sight.

Where are you now?
Are you already standing erect
in the jaundiced shadow on my right?
The rain has grown clearer, harder.

Isn't the child biting the rain?
Over there, a man I know has a sizzling throat.

I think I'll go out in the hall now.
Will you go back and forth ten times with me?
Will you, with your large, white, bare feet,
walk with me
on the cold boards there?

12 May 1922

Rest

In the upper stratum of that resplendent space
bloom *kinpōge*
    (these are superior *buttercups*
    but they are not so much butter as sulphur and honey)
and below there are pearlworts and parsley.
Toy dragonflies made of tin are flying,
and the rain crackles
    (an oriole calls   calls
    besides there's even a silverberry)
I throw myself out in the grass,
and the clouds have both white spots and black spots,
everything glittering, boiling.
I take my hat and throw it down, and there a black mushroom
    tophat.
I lean backward, puffing my chest up, and my head goes to the
    other side of the mound.
I yawn,
and in the sky too a devil appears and shines.
    These dead grasses are soft,
    now this, an ultimate cushion.
The clouds have all been plucked,
and the blue has turned into a giant net.
That's the gleaming mineral plate.
    The oriole does his thing incessantly,
    and a skylark falls toward me, crackling

14 May 1922

■☐ Annelid Dancer

(Yes, it's water sol,
it's opaque agar liquid)
Sun's a golden rose.
A red, tiny wormy worm,
draping itself with water and light,
is dancing a solitary dance
(Yes, $\delta \gamma e \, 6 \, \alpha$
in particular, arabesque ornate letters)
the corpse of a winged insect
a dead yew leaf
pearly bubbles and
a torn rachis of moss
(Red, tiny princess dear
now above the bottom in the deep
dances, yes she dances all alone
only with a yellow fluff;
no, but soon, it'll be soon,
up she'll come in no time at all)
The red annelid dancer
with two pointed ears,
each metamere, phosphorescent, coral,
correctly adorned with a pearly button,
turns round and round, pirouetting
(yes, $\delta \gamma e \, 6 \, \alpha$
in particular, arabesque ornate letters)
With her back glistening
pirouette she does with all her might,
but her pearls, in truth, are all fake,

not even glass, but gassy beads
    (no, but even so,
    δγe6α
    in particular, arabesque ornate letters)
With her back glistening
dance she does with all her might, or so I say.
But if, in truth, you leap about, tortured by bubbles clinging,
all that isn't easy for you.
    Besides, the sun has set behind the clouds;
    I got pins and needles, sitting on a stone;
    the black wood chip at the bottom of water looks, I say,
        like a caterpillar or a sea cucumber.
    Besides, first of all, I can't see your shape.
    Have you really melted away, I wonder.
    Or, was all this an opaque blue dream
    from the start, I wonder
    (No, she's there, she's there,
    princess dear, she's there
    δγe6α
    in particular, arabesque ornate letters)
Humph, water's opaque,
light's at a loss,
worm's *δγe6α*
    in particular, arabesque ornate letters, you say,
    oh you make me ticklish
(yes, I'm quite certain about that, sir
    δγe6α
    in particular, arabesque ornate letters)

20 May 1922

44

■▭ "The hard *keyura* jewels..."

The hard *keyura* jewels hang straight down.
Twirling, shining, the creatures keep falling.

Truly, they are the angels' cries of grief,
clearer than hydrogen—
haven't you heard them
sometime, somewhere?
You must have heard their cries
stab heaven like icy spears.

But if you hear of the people who fall,
or of the people who, drowning,
try to swallow the bitter salt-water,
you, as you are now, will merely think
it's a piteous story about some foolish people,
or a story a little unusual.

But to merely think that
and to actually bite the water
are totally, wholly different.
The water is so cold it feels hot,
so bitter it seems tasteless,
so painful it penetrates the blue dark.

All who fall there cry,
"Did I fall in this lake?
Is it possible that I should have fallen?"

Yes, who'd believe it, at first?
And yet finally they will believe it
and feel all the more sorrowful.

I have told you this
not to prevent you from falling,
but so you'll swim across it when you fall.
For everyone sees,
and the strongest fall by their wish
and then soar with others.

21 May 1922

◼▭ Koiwai Farm

Part 1

I got off the train very quickly.
So quickly that a cloud glinted.
But there's someone who's even quicker.
Someone who looks much like Mr. Furukawa, of Chemistry.
In that olive jacket
he's a quiet Bachelor of Agriculture.
A while ago, at the station in Morioka
I'm sure that's what I thought.
When he steps out of sugar water
the cold, bright waiting room
        . . . so do I.
A horse cart stands there.
The driver says something.
It's a splendid horse cart, painted black.
A matte-finish.
The horse is excellent, too, a hackney.
The man gives a slight nod
and as casually as if
he were hoisting himself up, a small load,
he climbs onto the cart and takes his seat
        (crossing of scant light)
His back, in the sun, blue,
is bent forward a little, hushed.
I walk to the horse and stand by it.
This could be a passenger coach.
Doesn't look like the farm's.

If so, they ought to ask me at once,
Coming with us?
The driver ought to call out from his side.
I don't have to have a ride,
I'm going to walk twelve miles from here
and somewhere at the foot of Saddle Mountain
I'd like to have some time for myself.
The air is bright there,
trees and grasses are magic lanterns.
Windflowers will be in bloom,
lilies-of-the-valley in tight clusters.
To have time to stay there a while
I'd better have a ride at least to the headquarters.
Today, surely, even I
could use a ride on a horse cart.
And yet, look,
the cart is already moving
　　　　(This is the good thing:
　　　　that while you're thinking what to do
　　　　it passes by and disappears.)
It flits past my side.
The road is coal-black humus,
after rain it has some give.
The horse, ears erect,
tips pointed against the blue light,
jogs away, truly easygoing.

Now, as if pacing them off,
I have put away, behind me,
all the new development buildings.

This land has been turned into a field.
Two horses, soaked with sweat,
poke along, back and forth, dragging a plow.
That's on this side of a soft, siskin-colored mountain.
There a wind blows mysteriously.
Young leaves flutter variously.
Far off, in a dark place,
Warblers are rumbling, rumbling.
The transparent, ultramarine warblers.
        (The true warbler, said Hans in a German reader,
        isn't a warbler.)
The horse cart steadily grows more distant.
Sways hugely and bounces.
The gentleman, too, bounces lightly.
Having already come through much of the world,
he's now someone sitting indifferently
at something like a dark-blue edge.
And steadily grows more distant.
Horses in the field, surely two of them,
also two people, unnaturally red.
Because of the light filtered through the clouds
they burn redder and redder.

Part 2

A clumsy tambourine in a distant sky,
it won't rain today, you can count on it.
But the horse cart, though it seems fast,
isn't that good.
All this time, it has only gone so far,

only covered the distance from here to there,
this straight road of volcanic ash.
There, just where the road turns,
ears of wilting grass sway
       (The mountain's filled with blue clouds, gleaming,
        the horse cart, jogging away, is black, splendid.)
Lark, lark
it's a lark that has just climbed
into the sky dotted with a million pieces of silver.
It's black, swift, gold.
Brownian movement in the sky.
Then, as for his wings,
he has four, like a beetle;
amber ones and hard, lacquered sheaths,
surely, it has them twofold.
Singing exceptionally well.
Swallowing the light of the sky.
Drowning because of light waves.
Of course, far off in the distance,
many more of them are singing.
They are a backdrop.
That must be why, from their side,
the one here looks very brave.
From behind me comes someone like a doctor
wearing this late in May
a long black overcoat.
Often seems to look this way.
That's what you very commonly do
when you walk on a solitary road all alone.
In winter, once, just like this,

a black inverness came up
and from a distance threw a buoy of words at me—
Is this the right way to the headquarters?
Walking as if masticating the bumpy snow-road
with great difficulty,
he asked forlornly—
Is this the right way to headquarters?
Because I merely, bluntly said, Yeah,
I felt, just that much, very sorry for him.
The one today comes from a farther distance.

Part 3

Already at the entrance: [KOIWAI FARM]
    (just as usual)
bushes crowded with wild roses and akebia
[WE HUMBLY PROHIBIT VENDORS AND MUSHROOM
                                     COLLECTORS]
    (just as usual   soon there'll be the hospital)
[SANCTUARY]   humph   just as usual
a small swamp and a stand of blue trees
in the swamp the water is dark and stagnant
again   blue phosphorescence of iron gel
over there in the field there are white birches too
white birches grow in Kōma and beyond don't they
one time I was saying to School Inspector Haneda
it is quite high here
the same as at Kōma after all
would you listen to these bird calls
what a great number of birds

it's as if I'd come upon a birds' school
it's like rain   it's like a bubbling up
there there there so many birds
such a number   sing sing sing
rondo capriccioso
gyukk gyukk gyukk gyukk
there's one at the core of the tree too
it's because of the sanctuary   it flies up
        (it isn't because of the sanctuary   gyukk gyukk)
not one   but a flock
more than ten   make an arc
        (gyukk gyukk)
a three-pronged spearhead   make an arc
blue glow blue glow a stand of alders
almost giddying   these bird calls
        (noise turns low in a blur
        because it's gone behind me
        or because of a warning rhythm
        it's both   bird calls)

Part 4

The smug headquarters building
stands this side of the cherries and poplars;
on its solitary observation deck
I no longer find
the Robinson anemometer's small bowls
or the quaking weather vane.
        The fine, matte-finished horse cart of a while ago
        by now must be standing still somewhere, as if forgotten;

the black overcoat of May
turned at some building and was gone.
In winter, on the frozen pond here
children laughed terribly.
Today in spring's scallion-colored water
willow buds already blur.
Beyond it, a field.
The field is dug up brown,
with stable-manure in a square heap.
Some witches'-brooms on the cherry trees lining the road
stick out little green flags,
among those hanging against curled distant clouds
there are some with fresh, warbler-colored light.
And yet those larks sing too much.
Even between the horse-breeding division and headquarters
there have to be more than a dozen larks.
This side of the line of sturdy, cultivated land
floating in quaking clouds,
short innocent electric poles
bending to the right, tilting to the left, terribly confused,
at a turning point, a single blue tree.
(Must be a birch. It isn't a willow.)
The cultivation division's not far from here.
Even during the winter, when the snow had hardened,
a horse sled managed to pass through it
(The snow seems not to have been hard,
because the sled had swirled it up,
certainly had blown up the sediment of yeast
into the lucid air current.)
That time, through the moves of glistening snow

I don't know how often I went back and forth,
whistling a precarious serenade
    (four rows of brown deciduous pines)
nevertheless, how well-balanced
that out-of-tune serenade was
with the winds and the snow that flapped up from time to time!
the same as ice cream on a snowy day
    (though, in that case, there'd be a fire in the fireplace
    the Muscovite would get burned a bit on the outside
    a luxury we can't possibly see)
spring Vandyke brown
the field has been cultivated neatly
the clouds today, too, are platinum and platinum black
in their dazzling light and darkness
birds are ceaselessly calling
    (clouds' hymn and sun's creaking)
and if you raise your eyes again
a gray thing a running thing a snakelike thing   it's a ring-
    necked pheasant
it is a zinc-coated ring-necked pheasant
because it passes vernally trailing an exceedingly long tail
another flies down
it is not a mountain pheasant
    (Is that a mountain pheasant? On a mountain? In summer?)
walks fast   flowing
in orange sunlight
the pheasant's sliding   flowing
calling.
So that's a pheasant call.
At the edge of the cultivated land I'm looking over,

54

on the blue grass hillock, four or five trees, confused,
what whimsical cherry trees,
all, ghosts of cherry trees.
Inside, a weeping willow
with ibis-colored blossoms
            (in the sky a clutch of platinum-sponge tears off)
step on the hangings of those glittering ice pieces
and thrust forward like a sword
into the hollow of blue-light heaven.
Now I am not lonely.
I'll live my life all by myself.
I'll press straight on, openly.
If you say that won't do,
tear off your country-style high collar.
If what lies farther ahead begins to turn too dark-blue. . . .
Don't think that far ahead.
Whistle as vigorously as you can.

Part 5
Saddle Mountain looks dark and very large.
Too lopsided to the west.
Snow once gleamed on that edge.
Surely, that is
part of the Mt. Nanshō and Numamori formation.
Definitely does not belong to the Iwate volcano.
After all, it could be
made of quartz andesite,
this is my discovery,
as I was once saying to Mr. Horikago

on the train
      (On the cobalt mountain ground to the east
      mysterious flames rising,
      in the rifts of train smoke,
      in the rifts of white clouds,
      I was observing cold heaven the silver plate
      like an absentminded god,
      that was on that train.
      Mr. Horikago deliberately frowned
      and put a cigarette in his mouth.)
Yes, he is a quiet man.
I'm always alarming
that straight, good soul,
always hurtling at him splashes of
something like a fierce white glow.
That isn't my intention,
it's quite the opposite,
but it always ends up like that.
What I mean, well,
all of it seems to end up
as something painful to him.
Today he's at school on day duty.
I'd like to get back quickly and see him.
At the moment, in the darkness of my desk cabinet
chocolate in silver foil should be flickering.
I bought it last night
along with some oranges
thinking that he would come to see me.
But of course he didn't.
That's just natural.

Yesterday afternoon, in the town's blue glow
I said,
Why don't you come to see me?
The tone was too fierce.
He was silent,
did not reply.
If you don't mind,
I added brusquely.
He turned color a bit,
his mouth closed, tight.
He'd thought to come
but then felt too constrained,
he looked disappointed too.
But I don't know what the matter was.
Look, where the mountain is, it blurs dark blue and gleams.
Come to think of it, for the last several days
I must have looked quite dangerous.
How pitiful of me to mess up everything,
to be lackadaisical in everything.
The black pine hill over there is Wolf Forest.
Truly fresh and *plump*.
That's for sure: looking at it on a map
it feels much higher,
but that's all there is to it.
Pass its right shoulder, and it's all downhill.
The elementary school of Ubayashiki will be visible.
I no longer want to trek all the way to Yanagisawa.
Trek all the way to Yanagisawa, get on the nine o'clock train.
Get to Hanamaki at ten, fall asleep tired, white,
white waves of tiredness, pulpy, wavering.

A five o'clock train would be just right.
Drop by at the school and change my clothes.
Mr. Horikago and Mr. Okudera are still in the teachers' room.
I'll take out the chocolate in tinfoil.
But will they all eat it?
Sure they will. At such a time
even I can't help feeling good and laughing;
besides, I don't have to worry about the chocolate
because it's neatly wrapped in new tinfoil.
But that five o'clock train doesn't stop at Takizawa.
In Takizawa the train stops only at one o'clock.
Shall I go back now? Go back swiftly from here,
get to Morioka probably about three,
and read that book in the waiting room.
No, that's terrible. For me after all
nothing's good but a wide place like this.
Outside the fields I'm always getting in someone's way.
I'll go to Yanagisawa after all.
In a depressing forest in a field like this
Beethoven with stolid black shoulders
droops his head in deep thought
or from time to time roaring, alone,
walks on and on.
His disciples follow him.
It's at the bottom of dark, dark mists.
Today that isn't so.
Saddle Mountain gleams too.
Well now, was there the cattle-breeding division
ahead of this, definitely?
I don't think I've walked through a place like this.

Cedars grow well,
it's a mild slope.
From over there, a flock of farm women comes.
Very neatly dressed.
Every one of them is tall and straight.
Their black kimonos are excellent
and their white capotes
harmonize well with the brown of the farm
and the indigo of the woods.
At the headquarters or at the cultivation division
there's got to be an exceptionally reliable engineer.
The sky has become quite heavy.
But it's gleaming white.
From the cultivation division the sound of a western-style bell.
It's faint but I can hear it clearly.
They've already come close.
I'll ask them, I don't have a watch,
"Is that the twelve-o'clock bell?"
"Yes, that's right."
They are all replying quietly.
This is just like an opera, isn't it.
In the manner of statues that have begun to move,
quietly looking this way,
correctly they all pass by me.
They walk toward the bell.
Classicism belongs to Greece, and brightness of hours.
I can already see the barns of the cattle-breeding division.
No cattle are out.
And I don't know if they're in the barns, either.
Green rows of larches and brown of the field.

Hushed.
At the bottom of sunlight, it's always hushed.

Part 6

The road has suddenly become vague.
There are larches, and grass is short,
indeed, it's a model field,
but if the road, which is supposed to take me to Ubayashiki,
drawn clearly on the map as well,
is like this
I feel a bit uneasy,
though if you decide upon your direction and go,
it's not impossible to get there.
To tell the truth, I'm a bit pressed today.
I must think about
Mr. Horikago, too.
There again, a field being plowed.
A white hat is climbing up its mild incline.
Though the hat gleams, is excellent,
it isn't, after all, in keeping
with this sort of western-style farm.
But possibly that person
may be going to Ubayashiki.
Not at all, she's working.
Besides, in the pine grove beyond,
though it may not be Wolf Forest yet,
there's quite a big road.
You take that one, there's no way to get lost.
I will—but look at that!

A dam there,
willows growing higgledy-piggledy,
and near the dam, only several yards of
road, neatly made.
A bit odd, what's the matter?
Well, this too has got to be a piece of
the farm's whimsical work.
For one thing, well, it can be a landmark.
In any case, cross it, climb that slope.
A considerable jungle of pines.
Though the incline's mild and it's nothing, a short slope,
it's not easy to go up.
I haven't slept well the last two nights
and I am tired after all.
Because of my tiredness, I perceive a tub.
What in the world is this association!
And yet, surely, this tub
still smells of pine resin, and,
brand-new, it's a small blomp-blomp tub.
A considerable jungle of pines.
Looks dark and damned lonely.
The clouds have come down quite low.
Ah yes, this is common—you climb up the whole thing,
there's another hill right behind it,
pines growing higgledy-piggledy.
But something bothers me.
The road becomes vague again,
grass ears sloshy, sloshy,
while over there, an excellent road
crawls north along the bank.

The right road would seem to be that one.
This one, the road on the map.
Supposed to come out at the connection to Akasaka.
It'll end up going too far to the east.
Shall I go over to the other road?
That isn't clear, either.
Saddle is beyond light and isn't visible,
besides, in Ubayashiki, definitely
the dogs will bark, will bark.
It depends, maybe they won't.
Here's withered grass, something's crackling.
It's begun to fall, begun to fall.
But the beads of rain aren't visible.
Just that the sky's glistery.
Not one bead falls on my face, either.
Still, it is crackling.
The grasses are bending their bodies.
It's rain. Definitely. Just as I thought.
It's begun to fall. I'll turn back.
Get on the train, soaking wet.
Get to the school by five-thirty.
Teachers' room, the dark blue space.
Chocolate and chairs
      (How is it that I have become
      as lowly as this?
      Those who are transparent, those who burn,
      those who climb at the end of the atmospheric strata,
      out of breath, praying,
      now they hide themselves from me.)
Shall I go through Onigori to Morioka?

No, after all, the earlier the better.
Best to get out at the station in Koiwai.
OK I'll turn back. This time too, I give up.
Hey, Yanagisawa!
Saddle, though I can't see you, goodbye!
Turn back, turn back.
A jungle of small pines, dark and full of bamboo grass.
But shall I take shelter from the rain a while?
The bamboo grass crunches, withered.
Besides, a temptation lives in the pine grove.
Though, now, that's nothing.
That's nothing, and yet
the rain leaks through after all.
I can sit on the bamboo grass if I want to,
but if that doesn't help me from the rain, it won't do.
Best to walk on and on, no matter what.

Part 7

A kite-brown field leisurely inclines
and is washed with transparent beads of rain.
At its feet a farmer in a white hat stands,
looks up reflectively at the clouds in the sky,
now, starts walking slowly
        (just like a traveler wearied of pressing on)
I'll ask him the train schedule.
Here it's a squelchy blue marsh
with sundews growing
        (Their light-red hairs are curled, and
        in some swamp where cattails grew

the horses of the cavalrymen under Marshall Ney's command
stepping foot-deep into mud
puffed, crossed it, marched forward.)
The clouds white, that man is waiting for me.
Can't wait any longer and starts walking.
From a height of topaz rain
come two girls wearing ponchos.
Red cloths on their heads in Siberian fashion
they come, straight toward me, hurrying,
Got to be the Robin sisters, got to be coming to work.
The farmer, like a courier viewing Mt. Fuji,
stands, waiting, hat tilted,
with white gloves on. Only sixty feet left,
don't start walking for a while.
Thinking that even if he waited
it would be embarrassing if it were for nothing
he sways and quakes like that
        (blue grass tips are last year's)
he sways and quakes like that.
Because the air's good and his face is completely visible
I can talk to him from here.
Take off your chapeau (black woolen cloth, wet too).
This person is already about fifty
        (May I ask you a question?
        What time's the train for Morioka?)
        (Three o'clock, isn't it?)
A person with a very sad face.
It's among the Nō masks in the museum,
it has some feeling of a hawk.
In the cold, white sky behind him

a real hawk cuts the wind, buzzing.
Under the mica-print clouds that drop the rain,
placed in a field, two carts.
This person is already about to go.
The white seeds are oats
  (Sowing oats?)
  (Yeah, that's what they're doing down there.)
This old man fears something.
Thinks there's something there
that's extremely frightening, terrible.
Nothing there but the horseless manure carts
and rugged, galloping, rat-colored clouds.
What he's afraid of,
as usual, is it the bismuthic labor?
  (You did put in manure.
  Compost and superphosphate?)
  (Yeah, right.)
  (It's a very pleasant place.)
  (Huh.)
This man is somehow
very reluctant to talk with me.
Is it because, by the two carts,
the skyline at the end of the fields,
this side of the quaking sky,
a tall, slightly round-shouldered man
in a black overcoat
is standing, with his gun ready, in the rain clouds—
is it that he's a bit touched in the head
and may suddenly turn his gun toward us?
or something about the Robin sisters,

or is it both, I wonder?
Don't worry, sir,
I'm afraid of neither.
There, there they are, in the sky, the birds
    (What do you call those birds, in this area?)
    (Dowitchers.)
    (You call them dowitchers.)
    (Yeah, they often come out when it's cloudy.)
Larch buds chrysoprases,
The shooter this side of the galloping clouds
again importantly readies his gun
    (When's the next one after three o'clock?)
    (Five o'clock maybe. Don't know for sure.)
Burlap bags of superphosphate of lime,
solubility 19, written on them.
The school's is 15%.
It's raining, and my yellow work clothes, too, get wet.
In the distant sky those dowitchers,
mouths wide open, make noise like beer bottles,
the mucous membranes of their gray throats exposed to the wind,
cutting the rain remarkably.
On the dead grass and raindrops
with a few pearlworts mingling in them
the girls of a while ago are asleep
covering themselves with thick ponchos of linden bark.
The old man's already gone off,
the shooter angrily squares his shoulders and readies his gun
    (cold motors of dowitchers. . . .)
dowitchers bleating—
what in the world is he trying to shoot?

From the direction the old man left in
comes a young farmer;
face red, freshly fat,
stooping his round shoulders Cecil Rhodes style,
he collects empty phosphate bags as he comes;
wears two of them neatly over his shoulders
     (It's raining, terrible, isn't it?)
     (It's OK, it'll soon clear up.)
Making a fire.
Can see red flames flickering.
The farmer's going back, I'll follow him that way.
One of the girls gets up, cleanly smiling.
Everyone's sound asleep in the bright rain
     (('Cause you are a good woman!))
Suddenly the farmer roars in such a loud voice,
blushes crimson and laughs like a stone mortar—
he must be much younger than I thought.
The fire's burning, transparent.
Smoke of blue carbon rises.
I'd like to warm myself a bit
     ((May I warm myself?))
     ((Sure. Come warm yourself.))
     ((Is the train at three o'clock?))
     (Three-forty.
     It isn't one o'clock yet.)
The fire burns better in the rain.
Der Freischütz is in the silver sky.
The dowitchers make noise, make noise.
I'm completely soaked. I'm cold. I'm shaking.

Part 9

Those transparent, swaying things are
the four agile cherry trees of a while ago.
I'm aware of this
but my eyes haven't seen them clearly.
Outside my senses, to be sure,
a cold rain is pouring
    (When I tread the stones that float,
        lost in heaven's gleams,
        Julia, rain comes down the harder,
        Cassiopeia turns)
Julia's walking on my left.
Her indigo eyes, large, noble,
Julia's walking on my left.
Pempel's on my right.
Zwiegel turned away a while ago,
turned away at the row of larches
    ((When fantasy bears down on you
        that's when a man breaks down))
I am walking, eyes clear, open,
Julia, Pempel, my distant friends,
I have not seen for so long
your enormous, snow-white, bare feet.
How I looked for your old footprints
on the ancient sea coast of Cretaceous shale
    ((Too much of a fantasy))
What am I so frightened of?
When you feel lonely, no matter what you do,
this is what happens, whoever you are.

Today, because I see you,
I don't have to run away, blood-spattered,
from a page of this enormous journey
    (Are there larks or not?
    Out of humus, wheat grows
    rain falls ceaselessly)
Yes, you are right, this part of the farm
looks quite mysterious.
Somehow I'd like to call it
der heilige Punkt.
Take this past winter
when I came to the cultivation division on business:
in the fragrant blizzard
I felt somehow holy, and,
almost freezing to death, I was walking back and forth,
back and forth.
It was the same a while ago.
Where do they come from, those children wearing *keyura?*
    ((Don't be deceived by things like that.
    Different things are in different spaces.
    Besides, don't you realize that for some time you've been thinking
    exactly like a copperplate engraving?))
In the rain, larks are singing.
With your flat, bare, enormous feet gleaming
white as seashells, you will tread
the field filled with red agate thorns.
    I've decided. Don't go that way.
    None of these things are right,
    they are dregs of light turned sour,
    cast from your religion

which, because you are tired, has changed its form.
In the perplexing enormous cosmos of imagination
where you can't measure your tiny self,
if you burn with righteous yearnings
and wish to achieve true well-being
with all people and phenomena,
if that is a religious emotion,
when, broken or exhausted by such yearning,
you desire to go, complete and eternal,
with one other soul only,
that transformation is love.
And if, unable to keep that direction,
you attempt by force and deception
to gain the essential part of love,
that tendency is lust.
Following the various processes in all such gradual changes
various visible and invisible kinds of beings exist.
This proposition, reversible and yet correct,
is terrifying to me.
But, however terrifying,
if true, it can't be helped.
So open your eyes, rise anew
from these phenomena of reality
that are visible to anyone
and that clearly follow the laws of physics.
When bright rain is pouring so hard
the horse cart moves, the horse is wet, black.
The man is standing on the cart.
I am no longer lonely.
No matter how many times I say I'm not lonely

I'm sure I'll be lonely again.
But, for now, this is all right.
Burning loneliness and sorrow,
the man moves in a transparent orbit.
Larix, larix, more blue,
the clouds more curled, gleaming.
The road turns exactly to the east.

21 May 1922

■□ Report

The fire we made such a fuss about turned out to be a rainbow.
Already for one full hour it has maintained a dignified arch.

15 June 1922

The Landscape Inspector

That forest
has too much verdigris piled into it.
I might overlook it if the trees were in fact like that,
and it may be partly due to the Purkinje effect,
but how about
arranging to have the clouds send a few more olive-yellow rays?

Ah what a commendable spirit!
The frock coat shouldn't only be worn
in the stock exchange or parliament.
Rather, on a citrine evening like this,
in guiding a herd of Holsteins
among pale lances of rice,
it is most appropriate and effective.
What a commendable spirit!
Yes, his may be beancake-colored, tattered,
and a trifle warm,
but the serious manner in which he stands erect,
such a pious man in the landscape,
that's something I have never seen before.

25 June 1922

■□ An Impression

The blue of the larix
comes both from the freshness of the trees
and from the nature of the nerves.
The indigo gentleman in the touring car
wearing a leather belt with an X-shaped buckle
stood transparent and erect,
his face pale as if from an illness.
He was looking at a mountain of light.

27 June 1922

Haratai Sword-Dancing Troupe

dah-dah-dah-dah-dah-sko-dah-dah
Under tonight's crescent in its strange garb,
your hoods adorned with cocks' black tail feathers,
flashing single-blade swords,
you dancers of Haratai Village!
Throwing out your lusty swelling chests
toward the hardships of Alpine farming,
giving your ample shiny cheeks
to the highland's wind and light,
clothed in linden bark and ropes,
atmospheric warriors, you, our friends!
The vast air stretching blue, deep,
gather the melancholies of oak and beech,
hold up torches over serpentine mountain ground,
shake your cypress hair,
and in the sky with the smell of quince,
burn a new nebula!
dah-dah-sko-dah-dah
Letting humus and soil chisel your skin,
muscles and bones roughened in cold carbon acid,
you masters have accumulated your years piously,
agonizing over sunlight and wind every month.
Tonight's the Festival of the Galaxy and Woods.
Beat the drums ever harder
at heaven's endline of the semi-plain,
make the thin moon's clouds reverberate
    Ho! Ho! Ho!

King Evil Path, of Takoku, of the past,
His dark dark cave five miles deep.
Going there is Black Night God,
His head cut up and pickled.
Andromeda shakes in the torches.
Blue masks a mere bluff,
Swords slashing, drown, drown!
Spider dance at the bottom of night wind,
Wearing stomachs, messy mess!
dah-dah-dah-dah-dah-sko-dah-dah
Make your swords meet ever harder,
invite from all around night's demons and gods,
even the tree sap trembles tonight, people!
Make your red robes flutter over the ground,
consecrate the hail-clouds and wind!
dah-dah-dah-dah
Night wind roars, cypresses in disarray,
and the moon rains down silver arrows.
Both winner and loser live as long as sparks
while the squeaks of swords last!
dah-dah-dah-dah-dah-sko-dah-dah
The swords are flashes of lightning, miscanthus rustles.
The rain of fireballs falling from the Constellation Leo
has vanished, traceless, on heaven's field.
Both winner and loser live a single life.
dah-dah-dah-dah-dah-sko-dah-dah

21 August 1922

◼▭ A Mountain Cop

Oh
what a magnificent oak!
A green knight,
he's a green knight wet in the rain, standing erect.

In the blue dark of the chestnut trees,
that long thing drenched, washed by splashes and rain,
could it be a boat?
Or a sled?
It looks too Russian to me!

In the swamp grow willows and salad,
I mean, a salad of pretty reeds.

7 September 1922

Lineman

Repairman of the capricious insulators of electric poles,
To you right under the clouds and rain, I'd like to give some advice:
The way you are, your form is right out of the Arabian Nights.
Bending your body, black, exactly like a hook,
the hem of your raingear wet and hanging mysteriously,
your repairwork that doesn't require you to move your hands busily
is too terrible a copy from the Arabian Nights.
If someone says of you, "He's leader of the Black Robbers,
or else the Devil
has pinned him up there,"
how would you propose to explain yourself?

7 September 1922

Traveler

You who go through rice paddies in the rain,
you who hurry toward leviathan woods,
you who walk into the gloom of clouds and mountains,
fasten up your raincoat, damn it.

7 September 1922

■⊏ Bamboo and Oak

You say you suffer.
If you do suffer,
when it rains,
you'd better stay in the woods of bamboo & oak
        (*You* get your hair cut)
Yes, stay in the blue woods of bamboo & oak
        (*You* get your hair cut.
        Because you've got hair like that
        you think things like that)

7 September 1922

■◻ Massaniello

Above the waves of pampas grass in the castle
is a made-in-Italy sky
where a flock of crows dance.
Several fragments of white mica clouds
    (moat, olive-velvet, cedars)
Are they silverberries?—glistening and swaying so.
Seven silver ears of pampas grass
    (below the castle, in the paulownia wood, swaying, swaying,
                                   the paulownias)
The red flowers of knotweed move.
Sparrows   sparrows
fly slowly to the cedars and enter the rice stalks
where, because it's by the bank and there's no air current
they can fly that slowly
    (because of the wind, the sorrow, I feel thick in the chest)
Is it all right
to call out his name repeatedly in the wind?
Is it all right to be calling it out repeatedly in the wind?
    (it's about time they came down the cliff
    with plows and ropes)
In the quiet sky where there are no more birds
again the crows enter sideways.
The roofs are oblong, their slopes shine white.
Two children run,
Japanese children flapping their *hoari*.
This time, parabolas of brown sparrows.
This side of the metallic mulberries

another child walks slowly.
Red, red are the ears of reeds.
  (it's Russia, it's Chekhov)
White poplars, sway oh sway
  (it's Russia, it's Russia)
The crows fly up again.
The flock of crows is zinc scrap in dilute sulfuric acid.
The sky above the castle is now white, Chinese.
Three crows slip down the cedar,
become four, turn and tumble.

10 October 1922

The Last Farewell

Before the day ends
you will be far away, my sister.
Outside, there's sleet and it's oddly bright.
From the clouds, reddish, gloomy,
the sleet comes down thick and clumsy
    (Get me some snow, Kenji)
To get snow for you
in these two chipped ceramic bowls
with blue water-shield designs
I flew out into this dark sleet
like a crooked bullet
    (Get me some snow, Kenji)
From dark clouds the color of bismuth
the sleet sinks thick and clumsy.
Ah, Toshiko,
now so close to death
you asked me
for a bowl of clean snow
to brighten me for the rest of my life.
Thank you, my brave sister,
I too will go by the straight way
    (Get me some snow, Kenji)
In your harsh, harsh fever, panting,
you asked me
for a last bowl of snow that fell from the sky,
the world called the galaxy, the sun, the atmospheric strata . . .
    . . . Between two pieces of granite

sleet makes a solitary puddle.
I will stand on them, precariously,
and get for my gentle sister
her last food
from this gleaming pine branch
laden with transparent, cold drops
that keep the white two-phase system of snow and water.
Today you will part with
the indigo designs of these bowls we've seen
since the time we grew up together.
Yes, today you will part with them.
Ah, in that closed ward,
behind the dark screen and mosquito net,
my brave sister,
you burn gently, pale.
No matter where I choose it
this snow is too white, everywhere.
From that terrifying, disturbed sky
this beautiful snow has come.
On these two bowls of snow you will eat
I pray from the bottom of my heart:
may this turn into the food of Tushita Heaven
and soon bring to you and all others
sacred nourishment.
That is my wish, and for that I will give all my happiness.

27 November 1922

84

◾◻ Pine Needles

Here's the beautiful pine branch
I took the snow from.
Oh, you almost leap to it,
pressing your hot cheeks to its green leaves.
The way you let the blue vegetable needles
sting your cheeks fiercely,
the way you look as if ready to devour them,
how it surprises us!
You have wanted so much to go to the woods.
While you burned with fever,
while you writhed in sweat and pain,
I was in the sunlight, working happily,
I was strolling idly in the forest, thinking of someone else.
Like a bird, like a squirrel,
you longed for the woods.
How you must have envied me!
Ah my sister, you will leave for a distant place before the day ends,
will you truly be going alone?
Ask me to come with you.
Ask me, crying.
Your cheeks,
how beautiful they are!
Let me put a fresh pine branch

on the green curtain, too.
Soon drops will fall from it.
And look,
it's fresh.
Can you smell the fragrance of turpentine?

27 November 1922

■□ Voiceless Grief

So closely observed by people
here you still must suffer.
When I deliberately leave the power of the great faith,
losing purity and a number of small virtues,
when I walk in the dark-blue asura,
you are going, alone,
the way set for you.
When I, your sole companion in the religion,
step out of the bright cold way of devotion, weary and sorrowful,
and drift in the dark field of poisonous grass and luminous fungi,
where will you be going, alone?
            (Don't I look frightening?)
With such a resigned, painful smile
and trying not to overlook
the smallest expression on my face
you ask mother, bravely
            (No, you look fine,
                you look really fine today)
Yes, you really do.
Your hair is darker than ever,
your cheeks are like a child's, like apples.
May you be reborn in heaven
with such beautiful cheeks.
            ((But I smell bad, don't I?))
            ((No, not at all))
No, you really don't.
Rather, this place is full of the fragrance

of tiny white flowers of the summer field.
But I can't tell you this now
      (because I'm walking in the asura)
If my eyes look sad
it's because I'm looking at my two hearts.
Ah please do not turn your eyes away
so sorrowfully.

27 November 1922

■■▢ White Birds

((All of them are thoroughbreds.
Can anyone just go break them?))
((You've got to know the job terribly well))
Beneath old-fashioned Saddle Mountain
the tufts of field poppies stir.
Beneath the clear blue birches
several brown horses gather,
shine quite marvelously
 (The ultramarine of the sky in the Japanese scrolls
 and the *turquoise* of the horizon aren't rare,
 but the corona of so large an imagination
 is rare, in a landscape.)
Two large white birds fly
calling to each other sharply, sorrowfully
in the moist morning sunlight.
They are my sister,
my dead sister.
Because her brother has come, they call so sorrowfully.
 (This, on the face of it, is false
 but not wholly so.)
Calling so sorrowfully
they fly in the morning light.
 (It seems not to be morning sunlight
 but the afternoon, ripened, tired.
 But that's my *vague* silver illusion
 after walking all night to get here.
 For I saw the morning's gold liquid, crushed, molten,

rise from the blue dream, the Kitagami mountains.
Why do those two birds
sound so sorrowful?
When I lost my power to save,
I lost my sister as well;
it's because of that sorrow

    (Last night in the moonlight in the oak wood,
    this morning in the swarms of lilies-of-the-valley,
    how many times I called her name,
    how many times a voice, I can't tell whose,
    responded from the end of the deserted field
    and jeered at me)

it's because of that sorrow
but in fact, their calls are sorrowful.
Now the birds, two of them, shine, a white arc,
descend in the marsh there, among blue reeds
and breaking off, rise again.

    (Before the new tomb of Prince Yamato Takeru
    his wives lay prone and grieved.
    When plovers happened to fly up from it
    the wives thought they were his soul
    and bruising their feet among the reeds
    ran along the beach after them.)

Kiyohara stands there, smiling.

    (A real country child, shining, suntanned.
    His head, shaped like a bodhisattva, came from Gandhara.)

The water shines, a clear silver water.
    ((Come, there's water there.
    Let's rinse our mouths and go, refreshed.
    Because it's such a beautiful field.))

4 June 1923

Okhotsk Elegy

The sea is rusted by the morning's carbon dioxide.
Some parts show verdigris, some azurite.
There where the waves curl, the liquid is awful, emerald.
The ears of the timothy, grown so short,
are one by one blown by the wind.
    (They are blue piano keys
    pressed one by one by the wind)
The timothy may be a short variety.
Among dewdrops, morning-glories bloom,
the glory of the morning-glories.
    Here comes the steppe cart I saw a moment ago.
    The head of the aged white draft horse droops.
    I know the man is all right
    because on that empty street corner
    when I asked him, Where's the busiest section of the shore?
    he said, It must be over there
    because I've never been there.
    Now he looks at me kindly from the corners of his eyes
    (His small lenses
    surely reflect the white clouds of Karafuto)
They look more like peonies than morning-glories,
those large blossoms of beach roses,
those scarlet morning blossoms of beach eggplant.
    Ah these sharp flower scents,
    I insist, can only be the elves' work
    bringing forth numerous indigo butterflies—
    here again, tiny golden lancelike ears,

jade vases and blue screens.
Besides, since the clouds dazzle so,
this joyous violent dizziness.

Hoofmarks, two by two,
are left on the wet quiet sand.
Of course not only the horse has passed.
The wide tracks of the cartwheels
form a soft series.
Near a white thin line waves have left
three tiny mosquitoes stray
and are being lightly blown off.
Piteous white fragments of seashells,
blue stalks of day-lilies half buried in the sand.
The waves come, rolling the sand in.
I think I'll fall upon the pebbles of white schist,
hold in my mouth a slice of seashell
polished clean by the waves
and sleep for a while.
Because, for now, from the sound of these waves,
the most fragrant wind
and the light of the clouds
I must recover the transparent energy that I gave
to the morning elves of Saghalien
while I lay on the fine carpet
of blue huckleberries bearing ripe black fruit
among the large red blossoms of beach roses
and mysterious bluebells.
Besides, first of all, my imagination
has paled because of tiredness,
becoming a dazzling golden green.

From the sun's rays and the sky's layers of darkness
there even comes the strange wavering sound of a tin drum.

Desolate grass ears, the haze of light.
The verdigris extends serenely to the horizon
and from the seam of clouds, a variegated structure,
a slice of heaven's blue.
My chest retains the strong stab.
Those two kinds of blue
are both the properties that Toshiko had.
While I walk alone, tire myself out, and sleep
on a deserted coast of Karafuto,
Toshiko is at the end of that blue place,
I don't know what she's doing.
Beyond where the rough trunks and branches of white and silver
firs lie in confusion, drifting, stranded,
the waves roll many times over.
Because they roll, the sand churns
and the salt water is muddy, desolate.
      (Eleven fifteen. Its palely gleaming dial.)
On this side of the clouds, birds move up and down.
Here a boat slipped out this morning.
The rut engraved in the sand by the keel
with the horizontal dent left by a large roller—
that's a crooked cross.
To write HELL with some small pieces of wood,
correct it to LOVE,
and erect a cross,
since that's a technique anyone uses,
when Toshiko arranged one of them,

I gave her a cold smile.
        (A slice of seashell buried in the sand
        shows only its white rim)
The fine sand that has finally dried
flows in this engraved cross,
now steadily, steadily flowing.
When the sea is this blue
I still think of Toshiko,
and the expressions of distant people say,
Why do you mourn for just one sister so much?
And again something inside me says:
        (*Casual observer! Superficial traveler!*)
The sky shines so, it looks empty, dark,
three sharp-winged birds fly toward me.
They've begun to cry sorrowfully.
Have they brought any news?
There's pain in half my head.
The roofs of Eihama now distant, flare.
Just one bird blows a glass whistle,
drifting away in chalcedonous clouds.
The glitter of the town and the harbor.
The ibis-scarlet over the slope on its back
is a spread of fireweed flowers.
The fresh apple-green grassland
and a row of dark green white firs.
        (*Namo Saddharmapundarika Sutra*)
Five tiny sandpipers
when the sea rolls in
run away, tottering
        (*Namo Saddharmapundarika Sutra*)

when the wave recedes flatways,
over the mirror of sand
they run forward, tottering.

4 August 1923

Volcano Bay: A Nocturne

Dextrine, the green gold of young peas,
where do they come from, and shine so?
    (The train squeaks; I sleep, tired.)
Toshiko opened her big eyes and
burned by a fierce rose-colored fire
    (That high July fever . . .)
was thinking of woods where birds live and the air is like water.
    (Was she thinking
    or is she thinking now?)
The train's squeaks, two squirrels.
    ((This year, those of you who don't go out to work—
    suppose you take turns going to the woods?))
says an obnoxious Arab chief,
a brass scimitar at his waist.
One day toward the end of July
Toshiko said, quite lost:
    ((I wouldn't mind dying.
    I must go to the woods.
    I wouldn't mind if I moved around, the fever got worse,
    and I was dead—if it was in those woods.))
Like a bird, like a squirrel,
she longed for the fresh woods so.
    (Squirrel squeaks are a water wheel at dawn
    beneath a large chestnut tree.)
1923
Toshiko opens her eyes gently
and in a transparent rosy fever

thinks about the blue woods.
The sound of a bassoon comes from ahead,
the "Funeral March" mysteriously begins again.
          (The train's squeaks, two sorrowful squirrels.)
     ((Do squirrels eat fish?))
          (On the second-class train window, frost designs.)
Daybreak isn't far off.
I clearly see the trees and the grass on the cliff.
The train's squeaks have grown husky.
A tiny, tiny white moth
crawls under the ceiling lamp.
          (The train's squeaks, heaven's music.)
This reflection of daybreak light on Volcano Bay.
On the Muroran steam ferry,
two red lights.
The eastern horizon striped the color of muddy malachite.
Birches and boxwoods stand black.
Mount Koma, Mount Koma,
rises, covered with dark metallic clouds.
In the coal-black cloud
Toshiko may be hidden.
Ah reason tries to persuade me again and again
but my loneliness remains uncured.
A different space that I do not feel
reflects a phenomenon, which was with me until now.
That's what makes me lonely.
          (We call that loneliness death.)

Even if in the different glittering space
Toshiko smiles gently,
my feelings are warped with sorrow
and I can't help thinking of her, hidden somewhere.

11 August 1923

▬▭ Commandments Forbidding Greed & Desire

To wear oiled paper, climb on a wet horse,
and go leisurely, in the cold landscape, by the dark forest,
over the slow, ring-shaped, eroded hill, among the red ears of miscanthus,
would be just fine,
and to spread a black polyhedral umbrella
and go to town and buy refined sugar
would be an extremely fresh project
      (Tits cheep, cackle, cheep, cackle.)
That the shrub of coarse grass called rice
has acquired a salad color
which even Turner would covet
is, according to the Most Reverend Jiun,
a manifestation of the Commandments
      (Tits cheep, cackle, cheep, cackle;
      the then idle elite
      are now quite reliable administrators)
The gleams of the gray fireline
on the dark mountain sputtering out loneliness
are also, according to the Most Reverend Jiun,
a manifestation of the Commandments.

28 August 1923

Religious Love

When the coarse rice stalks have ripened into a gentle oil-green
and, as for the west, it's filled with such a dark magnificent fog,
and grass ears, a field of them, are agitated by the wind,
your poor feeble brain
is disturbed blue, to the point of dizziness,
and your eyes, like Ōta Takeshi or the like,
are about to get gooey at the edges.
Your mind works so lopsidedly, pointedly,
and yet why do you catch from this transparent beautiful atmosphere
what burns, is dark, is obsessive?
Why do you try to grasp firmly in the human
what is obtainable only in religion?
When the wind's roaring in the sky,
and the refugees from Tokyo, half suffering from meningitis,
still come every day,
why do you deliberately take from the bright sky
the sorrow that shall never be cured?
This is no time for that.
I'm not saying it's good or bad,
I'm concerned that you're going too far,
I can't overlook it.
Come now, wipe your tears, collect yourself.
You must not love in so religious a manner.
That's where two spaces overlap,
absolutely no place
where we beginners can stay.

16 September 1923

Past Desire

Pale-blue sap oozes from the severed root.
I smell fresh humus
and work in the glittering air after the rain,
an immigrant puritan.
The clouds run, rocking dizzily.
Each of the pear leaves has precise veins.
On a branch with fruit-bearing blossoms a raindrop becomes a lens
accommodating the sky, the trees, the entire scene.
I hope the drop will not fall,
until I finish digging a circle here.
For, as soon as I remove this small acacia
I will politely bend down and touch my lips to it.
The way I look furtively in its direction,
in a collared shirt and tattered jacket,
shoulders squared as if I had a secret intent,
I may look like a terrible rascal,
but I think I'll be forgiven.
In the world of these phenomena
where everything is unreliable,
where you cannot count on anything,
the unreliable attributes
help form such a beautiful raindrop
and dye a warped spindle tree
like a gorgeous fabric
from rouge to the color of moonlight.
Now I have dug out the acacia,
I am content to lay down the hoe

and go under the tree, smiling generously
as if meeting my lover who's been waiting.
It is a form of desire.
Already it has become a water-blue past.

15 October 1923

Single Tree Field

As the pines suddenly brighten
and the field flashes open,
infinitely infinitely the dead grass burns in the sun,
electric poles gently relay the white insulators
on and on, to Bering City.
The clear ultramarine heaven,
a man's wishes cleansed—
larches again grow young and flare.
Ear's hallucination, transparent larks—
the blue rise and fall of Seven Shower Mountain
rises and falls in the imagination as well,
and the willow trees in a cluster
are the willows on the bank of the Volga,
hushed in heaven's malachite bowl.
Yakushi's yellowish brown rises sternly, sharply,
the crater snow bears a distinct stripe in each wrinkle
and Saddle Mountain's sensitive edge
raises nebula in the blue sky
           (Hey, oak,
             is it true your nickname's
             'tobacco tree of the mountain'?)
What a blessing
to be able to walk half a day
in such a bright vault and in grass!
I'd be glad to be crucified for it.
It's like having a glimpse of one's love
           (Hey, tobacco tree of the mountain,

you better stop that odd dance,
they might call you a futurist)
I am the forest and the field's lover.
As I rustle ahead among the reeds,
a green epistle, modestly folded,
gets into my pocket, before I know it,
and as I walk in the dark parts of the woods,
crescent-shaped lip marks
cover my elbows and pants.

28 October 1923

▪▭ Winter and Galaxy Station

Birds fly like dust in the sky,
heat haze and blue Greek letters
busily burn over the snow in the field.
From Japanese cypresses along the Great Passen Highway
frozen drops fall in shining abundance,
the distant signals of Galaxy Station
stagnate scarlet this morning.
While the river makes the ice flow away steadily,
the people, in rubber boots,
in fox and dog furs,
pretend interest in ceramic booths,
or size up the dangling octopi.
This is that noisy winter fair of Tsuchisawa.
     (Alders and blinding cloud alcohol.
     I wouldn't mind if a golden goal of parasites
     was hanging coolly there)
Ah, the light railway of the Galaxy in winter
that Josef Pasternack conducts
passes under many layers of feeble ice
     (red insulators on electric poles and pine forest)
dangling medals of fake gold,
its brown eyes opened proudly,
under heaven's bowl that turns cold, blue,
it hurries over the sunny snowy tableland
     (the ice ferns on the window glass
     gradually turn into white steam)
The drops from Japanese cypresses on the Great Passen Highway

burn and fall everywhere.
Their blue branches that spring up,
rubies, topaz, and spectrums of things
are traded vigorously as in the fair.

10 December 1923

▪▫ The Moon on the Water and the Wound

To stand under the blue gleaming sea of wide air
and burn in so obviously pious a manner
a white roll of tobacco
is to contribute to the negative of the moon's light and glitter,
to the cold moon on the water
      . . . but the wound on my right palm
          surrounded by the steel-blue isotherm
          throbs, throbs excitedly . . .
Hence, you should forgo the project of obtaining a piano
and play the medium-sized viola.
The pious, upright manner in which you stand
bathed in the ice crystals being woven in such light
is not appropriate for eagerly responding to
an ad promising a profitable company prize
      . . . But from my palm
        blood drips pale blue . . .
    a shadow of a bird flitting across the moon,
    the electric poles, the music box,
    the water gas biting the mudstone,
    and a black line of buoys
      . . . The blood on the palm
        freezing in the pocket
        perhaps emanates a faint phosphorescence . . .

And yet, if after all
you cannot take my advice easily
your solemn ecclesiastical posture
will be no more than a factory of anxiety under the air sea—
in a verdigris overcoat bought on monthly installments,
with a moist ruby fire,
raising faint blue smoke,
it will be no more than a factory of anxiety.

20 February 1924

▪▭ Untitled (14)

Trying to drink from the spring
you dropped your dog-skin glove in the mud,
but you shouldn't be so upset
splashing it about in the waves of pretty *cress*.
Look, the thatching villagers
smoking pipes, enjoying the sun
are snickering at you.

24 March 1924

■⬚ Rest

The whole sky is clear, warm,
except above the snow on the western ridge
where it stagnates, vague, white,
like a cloud in a crystal ball
        . . . chilled, sleepy, noon-rest . . .
There, dark cumuli
raise, like portraits, images of
the directionless *libidos* of
ancient troglodytes
while, on this side, flocks of larks
drift all over, singing
        . . . in the light, chilled, sleepy,
            the heroine of an old play pledges faith
            alone, lonely . . .
From the eastern peridotite mountains of ice and indigo
a cold wind blows down,
crosses canals one after another,
sings through the thorny branches of acacia
and grasses withering from their tips,
draws a mysterious curve
with three stalks of mugwort
           (eccolo qua!)
Through the wind innumerable dots of light float up and down,
and the group portraits of cumuli
now flow leisurely to the north.

4 April 1924

◼◻ The Weather Bureau

Shaman Mountain's right shoulder
has suddenly been covered with snow.
The highlands behind us too
are full of strange clouds,
extremely agitated.
        . . . The crop failure is at last upon us . . .
The cedars have all turned brown,
migrant birds have fallen, already many flocks of them.
        . . . Get me the carbon chart, will you? . . .
Now there are thunderclaps in the sixth zone.
The park is already
filled with townspeople.

6 April 1924

◼◻ The Crow

Under the ultramarine heaven
through the reflections of the highland snow,
a transparent wind is blowing,
moving the rows of dull brown larches,
each differently.
A crow, in the ultraviolet rays that burn him,
perches on the core extending unusually long from one of them,
anxious to remember
a very old yellow dream.
The wind passes continuously,
the trees shake precariously,
the crow, like a rowboat
     . . . he's rocking it himself . . .
drifts in the waves of the winter heat haze.
And yet the many snow sculptures
lie too quiet.

6 April 1924

■□ The Sea-Eroded Tableland

After the sun enters the sixth and final zone,
the sky grows totally dull,
the tableland hazy, like the sea of boundless desire
    . . . The sea the color of illusion
        sadly yet nostalgically
            bites into the chest of the spring of continence . . .
There, the snow remains in a design of wave crests
and the larch woods and valleys
continue their hushed rise and fall
into the feeble smoke in the sky
    . . . It's a sea-eroded tableland
        an old marker stone of kalpa . . .
Climbing an unclear path
a slow band of highlanders
who might be taken for exhausted, self-tormenting Brahmans,
trailing a shadow of horses,
disappears in the smoke of cold air.

6 April 1924

Mountain Fire

The blood-red fire
absentmindedly slides down the ridge
forms a monstrous crown
at the coal-black peak
lolls out a tongue of flame;
the agate needles shower
the willow's hair flusters
   . . . a dog barks frantically
       a lonely reflection on the marl cliff . . .
it changes into the shape of a corona or a torn lung;
under this horrible enormous night-flower
       (Lord, Lord, your eyes are stained with blood)
drunk, cursing,
the villagers return.

6 April 1924

▬▭ Reservoir Note

At the corner I have just turned
two poplars stand
and with strings of male flowers hanging quietly from them
float against blue ice-clouds.
Withered grass is oddly dark,
a small stream the color of mercury
flows as in lacquer pictures,
and at each turn
a thicket blurs as in smoke.
By now, the schoolmaster,
far beyond the blue fields,
must have finished snip-snipping his hair
and gone to bed, legs stretched.
Mr. Shirafuji the missionary,
emptied by his sermon,
must be sipping his bed-time tea.
No, all that could be last night:
maybe the schoolmaster is getting up with a dignified air
to write his next report,
and Shimaji Taitō's highest disciple, being so popular,
is walking intently
to catch the daybreak train.
Or perhaps
time's somewhere in between—
the shadow of my hat seems to suggest this last.
A Sharp pencil, the Moon-Mark,
a pale wind with the fragrance of beefsteak plant,

the moon in ripened cirri.
A silver hatchet, in the water or in my eyelids,
glints badly and shakes.
All day Takichi was cutting
a thicket of spindletrees
at one of the turns of this stream—
he must have dropped it on his way back.
Anyway the center of the sky
looks vacant, white, rough,
the wind is oddly sour. . . .
wind . . . and a twisted Judas tree,
the clouds over the sprawling fields
pale into mysterious stripes. . . .
I'll drop my pencil
the way a damson fruit
ripens and drops
and melt silently into the wind.
This whiff of fennel is it.
Wind . . . bones, the blue, somewhere a bell tinkles—
how long have I slept?
A blue star, solitary, beautifully transparent,
clouds, as if cast of wax,
dead leaves all look like birds' tail feathers,
and I tremble exactly like the leaves of the poplars.

19 April 1924

◼◻ Spring

Since it's her duty,
spring comes, blue, uncomplaining.
If the way she hurries in, carrying on her back
a rainbow spanning the whole town,
if that's childlike,
it's pitiful the way she comes right beneath
the clouds curled in the shape of a heron.
  (Bonan Tagon, Shinjoro!)
  (Bonan Tagon, Shinjoro!)
The cherry blossoms, in the sunlight,
somehow look like frogs' eggs.

27 April 1924

An Opinion Concerning a
Proposed National Park Site

What do you make of this lava flow?
Isn't it dreary?
I don't know when it last gushed out
but when the sun shines like this and the air whirls and boils,
it looks like a large kettle.
Even the snow at the top looks blue, cooked.
Well, have some bread.
Why don't you all
start a campaign
to propose this as a national park?
Possibilities?
I can assure you there are plenty.
Of course, I mean the whole mountain.
The crater, the hot springs, of course.
About Saddle Mountain, that goes without saying.
Let me tell you something about Saddle Mountain.
It was created long before the Great Hell,
you can call it Ur-Iwate—
located as it is at the edge of the large crater.
Now, set up a Hell here.
Make it charming in the Oriental fashion.
Put up a red fence of spears
with a scattering of dead trees to terrify them.
Behind them,
plant flowers here and there.

I said flowers, but they've got to be things like
thorn-apple, adder-grass
and black helmet-robber,
you know, devilish things.
Then, when all's done,
and villains and scoundrels
gather from all over the world,
shave their heads.
Here and there, you build gates with stones.
You should have cuckoos over the mountain paths to Death,
wading across the Styx,
the crossroads of the Six Realms,
from Yama's Courthouse to the Womb-Trip—
through these, pull them around, barefoot.
Then, as a token of the remission of sins,
get them to buy false Indulgences to Heaven.
At the end, they'll see the Three Forests,
and that's where you play a symphony:
first movement, allegro con brio, as if leaping,
second movement, andante, as if groaning a bit,
third movement, as if grieving,
fourth movement, feeling of death.
As usual, first very sad,
then work up to ecstasy.
As a finale, blast off real shots electrically
from two field cannons
hidden this side of the mountain.
The moment they think, Here we go!
they'll find themselves in the real Styx.
But they'll first get preparatory exercises here

so they won't be confused.
Or for that matter, neither will I.
Now, have some bread.
The mountain there, Seven Showers,
an indigo picture painted on earthen ware—
see, you could use that as the backdrop.

1 May 1924

◼▭ Untitled (99)

The railroad and the highway
run parallel around here.
The electric poles cast bumpy shadows
in the fields already plowed.
The roadside trees, the pines,
lay their shadows neatly on the road.
In the small thatched stable
with a row of flowers planted on top,
a horse munches fodder.
A red-cheeked, barefoot child plays,
singing, pulling the three straw ropes
he attached to the stable door.
The willows flare against the blue sky.
The horses plowing the paddies busily go back and forth.
The smoke rises from grass fires,
and the mountains seem to flow, blue to the south.
The clouds shine quietly and break up.
The water tumbles softly on.
At the top of those glistening pines
a tall fire tower rises
and because the tip on one side is broken
a small russet-haired *goblin*
sits there and rests.
Resting, he looks around.
Far in the distance, where wind collapses,
gentle birds that feed on grass seeds
faintly rumble.

Just then, billowing silver smoke,
cleaving the air like a wedge,
an express train appears.
It runs very fast
but since each turning wheel is visible
the red-cheeked barefoot child
looks only at the train's feet,
holding the straw ropes behind him.
As the black train passes,
the giant man shouldering a three-pronged plow,
a long-time resident of the country,
stares after it with a silly grin.
Then he limps across the track to this side
and suddenly disappears, as if by magic.
The water again tumbles on
and the horse resumes munching.

6 May 1924

The Horse

After working one whole day among mugwort,
the horse, rotting like a potato,
feeling the juice of the bright sun pouring
on his rumpled head crusted with edible salt,
crunched, crunched, crunched on bear bamboo
at the edge of the field.
When the blue night came at last,
he returned to his stable
where, as if a high-voltage wire caught him,
suddenly he went wild, a mute struggle.
Next day he was cold.
They made an enormous hole
at the back of the pine woods,
bent his four legs,
and slowly put him down into it.
They sprinkled clods of earth
over his bent head.
They shed clods of tears.

22 May 1924

◼◻ The Bull

An Ayrshire bull is playing,
rubbing his horns in the grass and ground mist.
Behind him, the fire light of the pulp factory
scorches the midnight clouds,
and beyond the low dune
the ocean, pounding, pounding.
Yet, because the brass-colored moonlight
seems like you could scoop it up and drink it,
the bull feels good.
Now he's playing, butting the fence with his horns.

22 May 1924

Mr. Pamirs the Scholar Takes a Walk

As the atmospheric pressure rises
the blue bulge on the horizon
which yesterday trailed clouds as disturbed as
solid forms of mercury
seems gradually to recover its level position.
And the quality of our land,
composed as it might be of *lapis lazuli*,
is not valued for its lack of elasticity.
The ground which, as one walks,
forms small dents
may well be compared to gel.
That was a dream long harbored,
first in early India
and in time in Hsi-yu countries.

This side of the volcano covered with shining snow,
in a square field where seeds have been sown,
what may be described as streamers made of shavings
are erected correctly, twelve of them,
distinct in the evening sun the color of ancient gold,
flowing variously in diverse winds.
No doubt, they are some device with which to repel birds
and I have no special objection to them
but the way they are placed correctly in two rows,
the long one and the short one occurring regularly,
as if to offer respects to the high mountain,
suggests some kind of sky-worshipping tradition
or a custom traceable to a mountain sect.

Whichever it is, no one would overlook this scene
as only a product coincidental
to a mere practical scheme.

At my phrase, 'the evening sun the color of ancient gold,'
your eyes assumed a reproachful tone:
Why seize on despicable gold
to compare to this solemn evening sun?
By the designation, however,
I meant not the dark yellow matter
currently in traffic
but, tracing far back into the past,
beyond the oceans of multitudinous emotions,
that which was vaguely suggested
by the bodhisattva Nagarjuna in his Great Discourse,
namely, that exciting thing
which should properly be called quickgold,
its virtues still exalted,
its phases extremely active.

Yes, that in the evening sun of Kucha as well
the birds flowed through the air
as smoothly as they do now
can be immediately pointed out
from the murals excavated there.
But whether the dragonflies called 'tooth dye'
flew in the blue smoke over the marsh
cannot easily be determined.

5 July 1924

▬▭ Spring

The air melts,
heron-lilies have bloomed in the marsh.
The young girls, all of them,
let their sleek black hair slip down—
their new indigo petticoats
and aquamarine spring jackets.
On the steps of the bridge to the platform
the old bandmaster in red-striped pants
reads from his score,
as if to say, "It goes like this, boys."
The mountains flow faintly like smoke,
birds, flocks and flocks of them, pass
like the seeds of swallow wheat,
and a blue snake flies through the light of the sky
on outstretched beautiful wings.
The train, Waltz Opus CZ,
has yet to show its white shape
on the horizon that quivers like a pudding.

22 August 1924

■□ "Spring" Variation

Various flowers' bowls and cups
as they open their august lids
and spurt blue and yellow pollen
some of it
falls, as it comes, into the marsh,
turns into whorls or stripes
and is quietly gliding, avoiding now here, now there,
the water stone-leek roots that poke out glaring green leaves.
Yet those girls standing on the platform,
one of them just never stops laughing,
all the others stroke her on the shoulders, on the back,
and do many things, but no matter, she doesn't stop laughing.

22 August 1924

Wind & Cedar

On each one of the cedar's greenish brown clusters
the dazzling white sky settles,
a wasp drones near my hot eyelids,
a wind blows, and a white building
    . . . . a white whistle a corkscrew . . . .
silver, pain, and a person who closes his mouth, lonely
    . . . . it looks like me, too
         this platinum-haired beast's dazzling focus . . . .
half-melted, sparrows pass,
remembering, the wind blows
    . . . . I try but can't sleep . . . .
       (come let your mother
       into your sleep . . . .)
the dazzling afterimage of cedar needles
a dot, the white silver daystar
    . . . . eyelids are hot, the orange fire burns . . . .
       (at least get to be a devil in hell)
    . . . . my lips bloom like a flower . . . .
once again dazzling white daystar
       :

       :

       (a blinker)
       (these got to be grapes)
    . . . . faint red and gold . . . .
       (hey gimme work)
       give me my work)

              :
              :
scarlet-coated railings
                 (a peasant would find a different kind of work;
                 you just it's true stand here
                 making fun of people)
the copper-colored torso facing south
hair, kinky, gets mussed up in the wind
it looks like an Indian wrestler;
is that the tree god of this enormous cedar
or perhaps one of the winds?

6 September 1924

◼◻ Cloud

You may say you came as fast as you could,
but it's like talking in a dream
like cheap wine
 . . . . leaning against a wet midnight charred fence post . . .
Come, brother,
answer me
out of the coal-black cloud.

9 September 1924

.

Harvesting the Earless Millet

For a while, dazed, they face the westerly sun,
then busy again, bend their bodies
and start bundling the piled millet.
      Beyond them, children laugh.
      Women too, diligently,
      appear and disappear in a field the color
          of ancient gold
          . . . all over the cliff a white fire
             of pampas grass flowers . . .
Then, suddenly, they take a stance
and as if manipulating, as if pulling the strings, begin to sickle ahead—
red millet poles, darkened, muddied
      ((kabeiii i
naraiiii i))
          . . . the miscanthus ears are so bright
             even the children get excited . . .
At the ends of the muddied, red anthocyanin millet
people work intently
          . . . knotweed blossoms waver in the wind,
             western clouds curl up, and wound . . .
      women too, diligently,
      swim in the dark sunset stream
          . . . a flock of shrikes swoops into the miscanthus
             a flock of shrikes swoops out of the miscanthus . . .
As if embracing, as if pulling the strings, they sickle ahead—
millet poles, darkened, red
          . . . along the rim of the field

an oily green row of hemp burns . . .
((dedeppoppo
dedeppoppo))
. . . here, another group of children
bring a board into the street
and jump over it singing . . .
The children across the field have already vanished
far beyond wind and sunset.

24 September 1924

Untitled (312)

Wet in soggy cold rain,
relying on the faint phosphorescence of clouds,
I am walking tonight in love
with some bright windscape
of who knows when, some season of plums.
Now at midnight
I count one after another
each one of the houses vaguely asleep
surrounded with cedars and yews,
drift in the fragrance of rice stalks coming from I can't tell where,
hear absently in a distant sky
the voices of tired crickets and mutterings of water
and footsteps crossing puddles and mud
I can't tell whether mine or someone else's,
and while the larches make the wind lucid,
and the silver poplars disturb the clouds, swaying,
madly in love
with fragments of the bright words
innocently spoken
by the people with beautiful cheeks
who burn the red flowers of Oriental poppies
and pluck black plums,
through the rows of coal-black pines
endlessly I've come.
Ah must I make up for myself
what I am in love with?
I ask, shouting loudly

to the eastern sky,
and from a black forest near there
a mocking hollow voice
returns a fragment of the echo.
If you cast aside what you're in love with,
soon you'll be in love with love,
I mutter to myself, desolate.
I turn to see where I came.
An afterimage of the rows of pines
gleams palely in the sky.

5 October 1924

Flower Petals of Karma

Night dew and wind mingle desolately,
pine and willow go black,
the sky fills with dark petals of karma.
I have recorded the names of gods,
and shiver violently, cold.

5 October 1924

Praying for the Good Devil's Absolution

Yeah I know that tomorrow, while it's still dark,
you've got to go to town with a horse cart full of charcoal,
but past midnight, in such moonlight,
you shouldn't be rustling about, hanging rice bundles up there.
Even far off in a field the color of thinned ink,
I heard the rustling.
You never know who might come with what complaints.
First of all, look,
look, over there,
the water in the paddies goes black like tooth dye,
the soybeans planted along the ridges start vigorous marches,
over the smoky thirteenth-day moonlight
a cross-shaped corona appears,
the sky takes on the look of a fish eye—
in short, things that aren't too good
are happening, one after another.
You'll be all right, floating up there
among the amazon stones of the gleaming northern sky,
hanging bundles with a snotty air,
alone with greed in the wind-swept field,
but your precious wife on the ground
is tired, grown soft like sour milk
and totters back and forth, her mouth pursed,
trying to give you bundles of rice,
hooking one at a time at the end of a log.
After all, this was a bad year for everyone,
except that your rice took a good turn during the drought.

138

Now that's enough. Jump down, go home,
and until birds begin to fly across the sky,
have a good, solid sleep.

11 October 1924

◼◻ Excursion Permit

Can you tell the random trails of wild horses
from the real paths?

You say, plantains, sainfoins,
but do you know what they really look like?

Can you pass by identical yellow hills
keeping track of them all?

Look at the firelines on your map.
How can you tell them from the ones made later?

Do you know what the underground stream is like
in peat strata?

Suppose you get lost anyway.
Can you rush home
through the oaks, withered scarlet,
and the big shrubs of deutzia and rose
following only the directions given by a compass?

Finally the sun goes down
and it may even sleet.
Do you still want to go?

I see, you do.

26 October 1924

Fantasy During a Journey

After the desolate catch and the drought
I have come alone
along the coast
over countless hills
and through fields of miscanthus.
Now as I doze on the sand of a wild riverbed
in the weak sunlight,
my shoulders and back feel chilly,
somehow uneasy, maybe because
at the top of the last dolomite hill
in haste
I left open the oak door
of the wood fence for pasturing.
Maybe because I did not close the white door
as it was,
the shining cold sky I saw there
and the chestnut tree with parasites come to mind.
Upstream, in the lattice of the layers of clouds
and cold rays of sun
an enormous bird unknown to me
faintly rumbles.

8 January 1925

▰▭ Wind & Resentments

Ponderous in fox-fur,
you snatch from the wind such ridiculous resentments,
things that look like brass plates,
and throw them at me;
can't you see that I'm hurrying
along the pine road in the snow
and the ruddy cypresses lined up in the graveyard are watching,
I don't have enough time to respond to them one by one.
Ha!
in the cold sky over the town
a black smoke flows, flows.

14 February 1925

Shadow from the Future

The blizzard drives hard
and this morning another catastrophic cave-in
   . . . Why do they keep blowing
     the frozen whistle?
Out of the shadows and the horrible smoke
a deathly pale man appears, staggering—
the frightening shadow of myself
cast from a future of ice.

15 February 1925

Drought & Zazen

While the muddy, froth-flecked water of the seedling beds
reflects the shadow of a tin-colored heron
moving vaguely from one side to the other
the frogs' all-night chorus
drones into a sleepy dreary morning.
Today too, there will be no rain.
Here and there on the ridges
near the paddies where they just planted rice
they squat, motionless
each weighing the same koan
repeated for the last two days and nights. . . .
In the blue dark beneath the chestnut,
over the water-trickling drain,
with the stelae, the Three Dewa Mountains, at my back,
and in direct view of the scene,
I calculate again and again
the number of days before the delayed rice takes root,
the number of days before bifurcation, and the time when the ears will
come out.

The stone is cold,
the thin cloud-strips grow lucid,
and to the west the row of rock-bells darkens.

12 June 1925

■▭ Residence

In the crescent-shaped village south of it
with a blue spring
and many abandoned houses
they say they don't want to accept
a teacher turned seed-collector
    . . . . wind's light
            and grass seeds' rain . . . .
Even daytime, barefoot and drinking,
those blear-eyed old men.

1 September 1925

◼▭ A Valediction

How the triplet of your bassoon sounded
you may not know. Its joy
innocent and full of yearning
made me tremble like a blade of grass.
When you clearly know and are able to command
the characteristics of those sounds
and their numerous arrangements,
you will do heaven's work, painful and resplendent.
While the noted musicians of the West
took to strings and keys in childhood
and in the end became famous,
you took to the products of this country,
hide drums and bamboo pipes.
Now, among the thousands in the towns and villages
who are your age,
perhaps five have your gift and power.
But every one of them, I say
every single one of them will lose
in five years most of what they have.
Either their lives will wear it down
or they will lose it themselves.
Talent, power, ability don't all
stay with a person.
(Even people don't stay together)
I didn't tell you
but in April I won't be in school.
Perhaps you'll have to walk a dark, hard way.

But then, if your power dulls
and your beautiful sound loses its rightness and brilliance
to the point that you can't recover it,
I will refuse to see you.
What I hate most
is the majority that rests in comfort
upon its mediocre accomplishments.
When you—listen to me carefully—
when the time comes that a gentle girl fills your heart,
an image made of innumerable shadows and lights will appear to you.
You must make music out of it.
While others live in town or waste their time,
you alone will reap the grass in Stone Field.
With that loneliness you must make music.
You must take all the insults and poverty, and sing.
If you don't have an instrument
—remember you are my disciple—
play, as best you can,
the organ made of light
that fills the whole sky.

25 October 1925

■□ The Highway

What's making that scratchy noise behind the wind?
I guess it's someone breaking firewood from the roadside pine.
It's stopped—
they must be listening to me.
As I pass by,
they stand around, looking innocent.
The younger boy, just a kid with round cheeks,
eyes me vaguely.
Suddenly his big brother poises a pole, looking up,
as if aiming at a bird.
The pole has a small sickle at its end.
The sky is cold,
the white mountains mushroom,
and as for the large pine,
oh well, the contractors will cut it down anyway
to add to the cost of the public hall in Morioka.

14 January 1926

■■▢ Spring

When the sun shines, birds sing,
the oak woods here and there
grow hazy,
I'll have dirty palms
that make a gritty noise.

2 May 1926

The Snake Dance

With this budding willow branch
let me tap him on the head.
Tapped, he slithers around,
so sensuous and clumsy.
He's no rattlesnake
but rustles his tail anyhow.
Item: though not of the tail-resounding species,
a snake may still make a noise.
Blue,
blue,
his pattern too is blue, magnificent,
a magnificent rhythm.
Yes, that's the pose.
The theme of this one must be
"White Attack."
Finally he opens his pinkish mouth,
an act comparable to the pose
the actor strikes, a little nervous.
Let me poke him a little more.
I have to handle manure today
so I'm fooling around with a snake.
But, snake,
teasing you
is like eating a sour tomato.
Are you getting out?
So am I.

20 June 1926

Field

A shower pours,
kicks up the earth, the dust;
 ah, bathed in the rising steam
 I'm alone, resent the work
  . . . dead leaves of fern
   a wild rose root
   around the tower that fell to pieces
   ants now run busily . . .
Cedars put on the streams of shower,
again cast up faint, white splashes.

15 July 1926

Flood

Under the malicious glints of the clouds
the Kitagami, grown twice in width, perhaps ten times in volume,
bears yellow waves.
All the iron barges are being tugged to the army camp.
A motorboat sputters.
The water flowing back from downstream
has already turned into marshes
the paddies on the dried riverbed,
hidden the bean fields,
and devastated half the mulberries.
Gleaming like a snail's trail
it has made an island of the grass patch under the pines
and of the Chinese cabbage fields.
When and how they got there I don't know
but on the warm frightening beach
several dark figures stand, afloat.
One holds a fishnet.
I recognize Hōsuke in leggings.
Has the water already
robbed us of our autumn food?
I climb the roof to look.
I hauled all the manure bundles to a high place.
As for the plows and baskets
I went in the water a few minutes ago, up to my waist,
and managed to retrieve them.

15 August 1926

Work

The corn is baking in the blue smoke,
pickled tomato is piled ready on my plate,
and the *chrysocolla* of a young cedar branch is close to my eyes.
Yet the breakfast that should be calm and enjoyable
makes me so uneasy.
I'm filled with anxieties about the manure
I threw from the horse cart and left on the slope yesterday.

27 August 1926

Distant Work

Beyond the miscanthus flowers and dark woods
some different specimen of wind is ringing.
In the lattice of glistering kinky clouds and blue light
the wind, with a mysterious fragrance, is trembling.
Reflecting the sky the river's empty
and a brick factory raises a bit of smoke.
From the table behind it
the echo comes clear, again.
Listening to it here, in the field,
it sounds like a pleasant, bright sort of work.
But at night Chūichi returns from there,
tired, furious.

10 September 1926

◼▭ Cabbage Patch

You stick a straw into the root
of each stolen cabbage
and call that Japanism, do you.

Rows of aquamarine columns
with entasis have
their Suiko-era foundations left—
when a straw is erected on each of them,
whenever a thief passes by,
it wavers in early winter wind, shining in the sun,
and surely derides him.
But you call that a victory
of Japanese thought, Iyasaka-ism, do you.

13 October 1926

■□ Hospital

On the way the air was cold bright water.
In fever, we become lively as fish
and feel very fresh, don't we?
The last cactus was burning, it was dazzling.
The streets and the bridge shone distinctly
and the people I met were all dressed
like the hummingbirds that immigrated to Iceland.
I imagine such precise outlines are not found
even among crystal forms under *microscopic analysis*.

4 November 1926

■□ Untitled (1015)

The buckets climb
and out of the leaden shadow of the *gauche* rectangle
brimming with waves now warm, peaceful
I come into the sunlight
and there   —a petal—
            —a sensuous shell—
        —a tuft of the helichrysum—
A moth lies flat
From the smooth powerful surface tension
struggling to separate its four wings
the moth writhes, writhes
            —here they go again, many tiny bubbles—
I must reinaugurate unto the ocean of warm shining air
this early lunger into the spring
the forerunner of lepidopterous swarms
A tiny cloud of spray
Scale-powder, bubbles, iridescence
The spring moth beats the water
and by itself flies
                up
            up
        up
and now sails through the brown tresses of cedars
and the indeterminate forms of clouds

23 March 1927

◼️▢ Cultivation

When we finally got rid of
the wild rose bushes,
the sun was blazing,
the sky was vacant, dark.
Taichi, Chūsaku, and I
wanted to fall just the way we were into bamboo grass
and sleep ZZ ZZ ZZ ZZ.
The river was carrying nine tons of needles a second
and a number of herons flew east.

27 March 1927

■◻ Sapporo City

The gray light avalanched in the distance.
Over the sand of the distorted square
I turned my sorrows into blue myths
and scattered them
but the birds would not touch them.

28 March 1927

◼▢ The Master of the Field

Through the fallen rice stalks and miscanthus,
across the water glistening white,
under the thunder and clouds,
master, I come to visit you
and find you sitting formally on the veranda,
listening to the movements of the sky and the field.
For seventy years,
every day, at daybreak and sunset,
you have cut mountains of grass,
you have worn hand-woven hemp even in winter,
so now your back is rounder than the pine trunk,
your fingers are crumpled up,
your forehead is etched with diagrams
of the rains, the suns, and the hardships,
and your eyes are hollower than the caves.
Every phase of the field and sky
has a duplicate copy in you,   .
and the direction of its change
and its influences on the crops
are muttered in your throat
as if they were the words of the wind.
And yet, today, your face is so bright!
After two thousand fertilizing plans
completed in the hope of rich harvest,
it is about time the flowers opened
pushing out of the ears of rice stalks,
but the fierce rain that lasted four days

and the thunder and rain since this morning
have felled the rice stalks in many places.
I think that tomorrow or the day after
if only they see the sun, they will all rise,
and we'll probably get the crop we expected.
If not, all these villages will have to face
another dark winter.
Against the thunder and the rain
I find words useless
and can only stand in silence.
Above the pines and willows
streaks of clouds trail,
and the gray water overflows
the banks reinforced so many times.
Nevertheless, the easy brightness on your face
bears no trace of the feeling you gave,
the year before last, looking at the summer sky
that had brought the drought.
Now, with the confidence you have given me
I am about to visit the village again.
As I leave, I see on your forehead
a cloud of uncertainty float up
and clear in a moment.
What it meant, I could never guess
even if I thought and thought,
going through a hundred possibilities,
but, dear master,
if it has to do with me,
even though my knowledge, all secondhand, is scanty,
even though I am as frivolous as a bird,

dear master, please look me straight in the eye
as intently as you can,
please listen to my breathing
as carefully as you can.
I wear old Western suits made of white hemp
and carry a torn Western umbrella made of silk,
but I am determined
to protect with my life
the Juryōbon of the Lotus Sutra
which, by the blessings of all the buddhas and bodhisattvas,
you recite each morning.
And now, dear master,
what heavenly drums reverberate!
what purity of light!
I bow silently
and bid you farewell.

28 March 1927

Ambiguous Argument
About a Spring Cloud

If that black cloud
startled you,
I'd say it's mass psychology.
A hundred miles along the river
tens of thousands of people like us
who plow the wheat fields
and shear mulberry trees
now turn their passion to fight the winter
to vaguely sad, nostalgic thoughts,
to faint hopes,
and, not knowing where to look,
cast their eyes to the cloud.
And that's not all.
That muddy, dark mass,
a catenary of warmed water,
that, I must tell you, is love itself—
the interchange of carbon gas,
mendacious spring sensation,
that, I must tell you, is love itself.

5 April 1927

◼◻ Forest

A Yorkshire pig, a large one,
cornered by the second daughter,
has turned into fierce golden hair
and, tilting worse than a top,
is running away toward the westerly sun,
along the hem of the black forest,
running blind.
A stick over her head, hair glistening,
a daughter of a village chief of the Japanese Nation.
Beyond a withering chestnut tree,
rocking, the evening sun.
The village chief in long hemp,
munching on something,
appears on this side of the forest,
shades his eyes with his hand
and looks up at the sky.

7 April 1927

Malice

With the black clouds swept together during the night
scorched by the sun climbing the mountains,
a ferocious, dark morning has come.
For the design of the playground today
I'll use the gray and red
that are on the hem of that devilish cloud.
I'll use something like
antirrhinum shaped like a fish with an open mouth
or base *hardy phlox*.
In this prefecture where there's nothing to eat
I'll pour a million
and will eventually come up with a devil's den.
This is a color scheme fit for it.

8 April 1927

▬▭ Untitled (1036)

Now burnt-out eyes ache,
the view they cover becomes twilled and sour.

Friends,
isn't the world
wholly made of blue fat?

11 April 1927

The Unruly Horse

Hōsuke's manure horse
suddenly rears.
Eyes scarlet,
it turns into a dragon,
tries to rake in the blue velvet,
the spring sky.
> A manure bundle tumbles down.
> Cloud beacons rise all around.
> On the cliff wall where day-lilies bud,
> magnolia flowers and the blue of the mist.
Hōsuke grips the bridle with both hands,
pushes the horse half against the cliff.
The horse struggles a few more times,
finally drops its enormous head,
gives up the thought of becoming a dragon.
"You have no right to keep watching
someone's horse go wild.
Your plow glinted
and that frightened him,"
Hōsuke says quietly, resentful,
bending over the spilled manure.
For the last two days
he's been in the dark stable,
tying up hot, sickening manure into hundreds of bundles,
and he's mad at the world.

25 April 1927

▰▱ Politicians

All of them want to make a racket
here and there and everywhere
so that they can have a drink or two—
      leaves of fern and clouds
            the world is that cold and dark
But soon
such bastards
rot of themselves,
get washed away in the rain of themselves.
What remains will be hushed blue fern.
And that this was the Carboniferous Period of mankind
a transparent geologist somewhere
will record.

3 May 1927

■◻ Devil's Words: 4

If you suffer so much from peace
I'll send into your home
the family surviving that execution.

13 May 1927

Untitled (1071)

We lived together
just one year.
She was gentle and pale,
and her eyes seemed
always to dream
of something I didn't understand.
One summer morning, the year we were married,
at the bridge on the outskirts of town
I saw a village girl bring flowers.
They were so beautiful
I bought twenty *sen* worth and brought them home.
My wife put them in an empty goldfish bowl
and put it on a shelf in the store.
When I returned that evening
she looked at me
and smiled a mysterious smile.
There on the dinner table I saw various fruit,
even white Western plates, among other things.
I asked what happened.
During the day the flowers had sold
for two *yen* exactly, she said.
    . . . That blue night's
        wind, its stars,
          the bamboo blind, the candles sending off souls . . .

The following winter,
my wife, without suffering,
as if withering, as if dropping away,
was ill a day, and died.

1 June 1927

The Prefectural Engineer's Statement Regarding Clouds

Although mythological or personified description
is something I would be ashamed to attempt,
let me for a moment assume the position of the ancient poet
and state the following to the black, obscene nimbus:
I, a humble official, hoping to wash both mind and body
in the vast air glimmering above this summit,
and in the cold wind passing here with a fragrance of roses,
and in the terrifying blue etching of mountains and valleys,
have managed from today's business schedule
a few moments
and stand here, knowing their full value.
But, first of all, black nimbus,
against my wish
you bring to mind an abnormal anxiety
and make me feel as if I were, in the words of the *Kojiki*,
"treading on air."
Let me explain, since you ask the reason:
For two-thirds of this past May,
obscene family of nimbus,
you covered the river and the valley to the west and did not move.
As a result, sunlight fell below the normal level
and all the rice seedlings grew excessively
or acquired red splotches.
Under the circumstances, as outlined,
I could not regard without grave concern

the season's rice growth in this prefecture,
I looked up at the skies and uttered anguished cries
more than several times a day.
Last night, however,
the veteran weather bureau chief
forecast it would be absolutely sunny,
and this morning, the sky blue, the air fresh,
I enjoyed letting my cigar smoke flow out the train window,
the fifty miles among valleys and twenty-five miles through plains,
happy to be on schedule. But now, past noon,
what deceit, what breach of trust!
As I scan the vast expanse from this summit,
I am gnawed by anger:
First that you, from here to the east,
disguised in the color of the nightingale,
cover the long stretches of land mass
to the limit of visibility
to rape the ocean;
second, that you rush northward,
going against those cirrocumuli
and the blue void;
third, that above the mountains covered with larches
you, dark atmospheric sea cucumbers,
are all too brazen,
now disappearing, now transmogrifying yourselves
into all sorts of lascivious lights and forms.
To summarize all this,
soft dubious nimbus,
although you allow me to enjoy several chinks of sensuous sunlight,
although you send me rude fragrance in the wind,

your intention cast out in the entire sky
with your gray black wings and tentacles,
your fluid mass of great baritone,
is too evident to hide.
Therefore, I, a humble official,
considering all the positions I occupy, public and private,
give you, these last moments,
a glare brimming with outrage,
ready to leave this summit
promptly, yes promptly.

1 June 1927

Untitled (1074)

At the very end of the blue sky,
above the atmospheric strata where even hydrogen is too thin,
there live a group of eternal, transparent beings
who'd find it too cloying
to think even such thoughts as:
"I am the entirety of this world.
The world is the shadow of a transient, blue dream."

12 June 1927

■▭ Raving

My sin has turned to illness,
I am helpless
sleeping in the valley sky.

At least at least
onto this body fever
this year's blue spear blades, take root.
Out of this humid air,
rain, be born
and moisten the drought earth.

13 June 1927

■▢ Colleagues

In those days when I had my desk
among yours, in this square room,
if on a bright calm afternoon like this
    . . . In the window, an acacia branch sways . . .
someone happened to visit us
with different ideas or dressed differently,
we would merely exchange casual looks,
faint expressions meaningless even to ourselves
    . . . The summer clouds collapse and shine . . .
but today, tired and weak after avoiding
the wasted fields and the villagers' fierce eyes,
foolishly, foolishly longing
for yesterday's comfortable address
when I enter this square room
your words and looks
become ten times as strong as your thoughts
    . . . The wind burns . . .
and strike me
    . . .The wind burns, grain stalks burn . . .

1 July 1927

A Rice-Growing Episode

Look, that paddy,
there's too much nitrogen for that kind of rice
so now we cut the water off
and don't do a third weeding
   . . . He came running along the ridges.
        Wiping his sweat in green paddies,
                he's still a child . . .

Do you have any phosphate left?
You've used it all?
O.K., if we have the same weather
for five more days,
pluck off all those
drooping leaves,
you see, leaves drooping like these
   . . . He nods repeatedly, wiping at his sweat.
        When he came to my winter lectures,
        though he had already worked a year
        he still had a bright smile like an apple.
        Now he's tanned with sun and sweat
        and looks gaunt after many sleepless nights . . .

And also
if at the end of this month
those stalks grow higher than your chest,
use the top button on your shirt as a measure
and cut all the leaf tips above it
   . . . Not only the sweat
        he's wiping his tears too . . .

I have already looked at the paddy
you planned yourself.
About the Riku-u No. 132
you did a very fine job.
The fertilizing was good and even,
and they are growing sturdily.
You used the ammonium sulfate too, didn't you?
They may say lots of things
but there's no worry about that paddy.
Four bushels per quarter acre,
that we can be sure of.
Keep on with it.
For you, true learning from now on
doesn't mean to follow dutifully
those who teach as a business and then play tennis.
Yours is the kind of learning
etched into yourself
in the blizzards, in the sparse free time between work,
crying—
which will soon sprout vigorously
and no one knows how big it will grow.
That's the beginning of new knowledge.
Now I must go. Take care.
          . . . May the transparent power
                    of clouds and winds
                    be transferred
                    to the child . . .

10 July 1927

The Breeze Comes Filling the Valley

Ah
from the south, and from the southwest,
the breeze comes filling the valley,
dries my shirt soaked with sweat,
cools my hot forehead and eyelids.
Stirring the field of rice stalks that have risen,
shaking the dark raindrops from each blade,
the breeze comes filling the valley.
As a result of all kinds of hardship,
the July rice, bifurcating,
foretold a fruitful autumn,
but by mid-August
twelve red daybreaks
and six days of ninety percent humidity
made the stalks weak and long,
and though they put on ears and flowers
the fierce rain yesterday
felled them one after another.
Here, in the driving sheets of rain,
a fog, cold as if mourning,
covered the fallen rice.
Having suffered all of the bad conditions,
few of which we thought we'd have,
they showed the worst result we'd expected,
but then,
when we thought all the odds were against their rising,
because of the slight differences in seedling preparation

and in the use of superphosphate,
all the stalks are up today.
And I had expected this,
and to tell you of this early recovery
I looked for you,
but you avoided me.
The rain grew harder
until it flooded this ground.
There was no sign of clearing.
Finally, like a crazy man
I ran out in the rain,
telephoned the weather bureau,
went from village to village, asking for you,
until, hoarse,
in the terrible lightning,
I went home late at night.
But in the end I did not sleep.
And, look,
this morning the east, the golden rose, opens,
the clouds, the beacons, rise one after another,
the high-voltage wires roar,
the stagnant fog runs in the distance.
The rice stalks have risen at last.
They are living things,
precision machines.
All stand erect.
At their tips, which waited patiently in the rain,
tiny white flowers glisten
and above the quiet amber puddles reflecting the sun
red dragonflies glide.

Ah, we must dance, dance like children,
and that's not enough.
If they fall again,
they will decidedly rise again.
If, as they have,
they can stand humidity like this,
every village is certain to get
five bushels a quarter acre.
From the horizon buried beneath a forest,
from the row of dead volcanos shining blue,
the wind comes across the rice paddies,
makes the chestnut leaves glitter.
Now, the fresh evaporation,
the transparent movement of sap.
Ah, in the middle of this plain,
in the middle of these rice paddies rustling as powerfully as if they were

reeds,

we must dance, clapping our hands, like the innocent gods of the past,
and that is not enough.

14 July 1927

■▭ Untitled (1087)

What a coward I am.
Because the rain at daybreak
beat down the rice stalks around here,
I work like mad,
I try to distract myself from the fear.
But look, again in the west
the black death floats up.
In the spring, in the spring,
was that not bright love itself?

20 August 1927

■□ Untitled (1090)

No matter what he does, it's too late,
he's one of our ordinary friends.
He reads magazines, raises rabbits,
makes all the cages himself,
puts twenty or so of them under the lean-to,
and their eyes are moist and red,
they eat cowpeas from your hand,
they even chirp like warblers.
And that too is too late.
No matter what he does, it's too late,
he's one of our ordinary friends.
He looks at catalogues, marks them,
gets gladiolas by mail,
plants them with labels
before a patch of *myōga* and a camellia,
and large flowers bloom, glaringly,
the old people say they're divine,
passers-by all praise them.
And that too is too late.
No matter what he does, it's too late,
he's one of our ordinary friends.
He buys mushroom spores,
clears the shed,
even makes a compost of wheat straw,
hangs a thermometer,
pours water every day,
and soon white champignons

poke out their faces one after another.
And that too is too late.
No matter what he does, it's too late,
he's one of our ordinary friends.
He puts on tortoise-shell rubber boots,
buys and wears an olive crepe shirt.
His cheeks are bright, hair kinky and pretty.
Still, for all that,
no matter what he does, it's too late,
no matter what he does, it's too late,
he's one of our ordinary friends,
he's one of our ordinary friends.

20 August 1927

▬▭ Member of a Committee to Judge Free-Style Paintings

Look here, this must be Kamchatka.
The house pillars and eaves are all dyed pink.
Migrant birds swirl up in the sky, like dust,
electric wires stretch quite boldly.
Children running over the siskin-colored mountain,
see the verdigris pines gallop over the hills?

This, I must say, is an authentic electric pole,
its insulators humming;
there's even a blurry robin perched on it.
The moon has an earthshine
and as a cuckoo flies past
the house chimneys cast up black smoke.

Come come come come,
this is really a fine tunnel.
Out of the hazy, peaceful ultramarine mountain
two rails abruptly burst forth,
spread out, almost hit your eyes.
Lots of birds are flying

while in the fields dandelions and milk vetch
roll out like carpets.

Aniline pigment flows out of the moon,
the sky is oddly bright.
Because the sun has set,
the three neck-shaped rocks spew rust, each its own color.
Small pines grow in paddies.
Along the wide, yellow, T-shaped road
a black figure walks, hair splashing, arms swinging.

When birds squawk along
and the snow falls white
everyone loves to go out on the ice
and play games
when birds squawk along
and the snow falls white.

As the sky pales in the evening
all of them in a row riding pale donkeys
cross with dogs
the field where golden roses glisten
as the sky pales in the evening
all of them in a row riding pale donkeys.

undated

Flowers & Birds: November
(Tohoku Chrysanthemum Contest: in Morioka)

(I'm saying, take the colors, for instance.
Once they read in an old wood-block-print book
a line like "Only the Right Colors, such as white & yellow, are valid,"
this becomes the golden rule
and they can never get away from it.
Now this just won't do.
When everything else is changing
and women & children think first about individuality
even in buying a single string,
the chrysanthemums can't follow
that 'White is for paper, yellow for straw'
kind of nonsense.
I'm saying, they should start giving prizes
to sophisticated off-shades
to stimulate the whole thing)
(You are quite right, sir)

undated

A Young Land Cultivation Department Technician's Recitative on Irises

Again separating myself
from the surveying group
I have come back over the beautiful green highlands
visiting on the way
dozens of dense, sensuous clusters of purple,
gatherings of irises fragrant in the sun.
To carry around pointed transits
and striped poles
trying to compete with ancient Kitagami for age,
to cut railways and paddies
and chip rocks
from a section of the semi-plain
that has stored days since the Cretaceous Period
only to turn out two maps—
that, under the azure vault,
is unequivocally the Original Sin.
Tomorrow, quivering motors
and huge plows shining dull
will bury under countless grooves
of overturned black earth
hundreds of these tall
pliant flower stalks
and each one of these petals and pistils
that look like silk or blue wax.
Then they will become dreary humus

and in time help grow coarse tough corn
and ears of oats,
but I, along with this clear south wind,
cannot but give the flowers
all my helpless caresses and boundless love.

undated

◼▭ "The man I parted from, below"

The man I parted from, below,
still with his brown horse behind him,
walks away along the bank,
trailing puffs of tobacco smoke.
This morning he hadn't smoked
but as he came to the mountain flats
the air began to warm and shine
and maybe he felt relaxed enough
to enjoy a puff.
For that matter, even the horse
seems to be limping, just as a joke.
The other side, refreshing summer grass stretches
down to Ubaishi and Takahi
and the light brown firelines
that hedge in at distinct right angles
make the highlands look
like a dozen or more playing cards spread out.
And there pass one after another
deep dark-blue shadows of clouds
and the aquamarine legs of winds.
The face of one of the cards
begins to brighten from one edge
and produces what look like
glittering red ants.
They are pasture horses turned loose.
The entire picture violently shakes again in heat haze.
The horses glisten, perhaps because

they twitch their chests
or flick themselves with their tails.
At the other end, facing the horses,
a man in white pants
with a small bush on his back
shakes terribly like everything else.
It's eleven o'clock in the morning
and he must be giving salt to the horses.
Many of them gather there.
If the smoking man's brown horse joins them
they might tell him, "You're too late, buddy.
We're done with today's special treat."
Or perhaps horses don't say things like that
but only feel them vaguely
along with the warmth of light and wind.
Bees buzz around me.
The crag where I stand and enjoy this perspective
grows faintly warm.
The west lies beyond the layers of hills.
In the Kitagami valley
gray mist collects and stagnates.
Above its upper edge, far in the north,
what looks indigo and monstrous
must be thawing Iwate volcano.
Right below it, at its foot,
Numamori and Numamoridaira
have exactly the same topography as this area.
And oh, when I stand alone on the lithosphere,
beneath a blue sky like this,
I feel a mysterious, helpless

love for our land.
Another cloud shadow takes over
and the herd of horses darkens.
The smoking man still clops on with his horse
going slowly along the great pathway
on the deserted flats.

undated

◼▭ The Landowner

When water rumbles
and birds, flock after flock,
float against the dazzling clouds and smoke in the east
and pass above the small pine field,
the man, liquor-bleared eyes red as agates,
wearing cattail leggings,
an old Snider slung across his back,
arms crossed high on his chest,
wanders alone like an angry ghost.
In the thin strip of mountainside village,
just because he has 7.5 acres of field,
everyone looks on him as a lord
and in fact he himself, though up to his neck in debt,
puts on the dignified airs of a landowner.
Behind him, continuous from the foot
of the Owl Wood and Mount Hexagon
extends an enormous hill, three miles square,
where chestnut trees, not yet budding,
gather their brown tops in tight congregation
and below it,
in the moonlight-colored grassland,
stands in the Oriental fashion
a wood of magnificent alder trees.
In such a pink spring,
his head sunk deeply on his chest,
the man wanders alone, desolate.
Because the rent rice he gets

is all borrowed again by autumn
(There's nothing left to eat, they say,
as they plead with him by turns)
he declares, Like a man
I'll feed myself on my own,
and goes off with his old Snider.
But when he manages to haul back a bear,
they say, "He killed the mountain god
so this year's crop is poor."
Though now the rice nursery adds to the green gold each morning,
the ferns along the ridges open their buds,
horsetails shine blue,
and here and everywhere
the people raise their tired arms
and plow dry paddies
with three-pronged spades that glitter,
he no longer knows whether
he should shoot a bear
or what other thing,
and, his eyes bleared, red,
paces back and forth like an angry ghost.

undated

Hateful Kuma Eats His Lunch

Facing the glistening river,
eating lunch by himself—
that's Kuma, no less.
Since I moved alone
into that abandoned shack,
he's been going as far as town to say,
"A ghost comes out of the woods"
or "A woman visits him every night."
He's that hateful Kuma, no less.
But today, it's not his game.
First, while sitting on the grass,
intently devouring his food,
he allows an enemy who hasn't once revenged himself
to pass behind him.
Second, he doesn't have his usual advantage,
my obstacle, which is mass psychology.
Under the azure, we are definitely one to one.
Third, he's vented enough resentment already
and has little hatred left.
So I feel sorry for him
and would like to avoid him
but if I did, he'd think I ran away.
This consideration compels me
to win today.
The river glistens,
and downstream, there's a noise of boats.
Kuma sits by a pine stump

shaped like a small table.
He turns and gives me a rude glance.
Then he gets so upset, really upset!
The yellow chopsticks he holds limply—
he opens them about 40 degrees
and with one of them
pokes at the rice stuffed in his mouth.
And of course I pass behind him.
Now behind me
the generalissimo is perhaps too excited
to taste anything as he goes on eating rice.
But I have won in so clear-cut a manner,
I feel dark blue, feel it's no good,
though I haven't done anything special.
He sowed the seeds as suited him,
he reaped the crop as suited him.

undated

■□ Night

When with hot palms, unable to sleep,
people still have had some sleep, from the old days,
gripping a crumpled towel,
or holding a black clay-slate stone.

undated

■□ "A few more times"

A few more times
I must glare at Kōsuke.
In the stinging wind from the snow-covered mountain
he decreed that the entire village turn out,
had a jumble of cedars and chestnuts cut,
had them erected,
two by the willow near the canal,
three along the cliff at the end of the woods,
those totally unnecessary electric poles
for totally unnecessary lights.
And now he says we'll have a completion ceremony
with the double aim of thanking the linemen,
he says we'll drink in the woods,
he says only the bosses will drink,
he says I'm one of the bosses.
Damn it! I'm not one of you bastards,
who trudge all day in a lazy pack
pretending to play truly important roles,
and instead of really trying to work
put on a show, saying
'The hole's too shallow,' 'The pole's warped.'
Donning his sooty boater carefully in this weather,
wearing baggy white pants like a silk dealer,
he's making a fire in the woods—such an ugly man.
I'll be damned if I won't go up to him
and glare at him again.
Yet, though I wouldn't mind glaring,

the cold wind with rain
hurts my eyes so.
Besides, for the last few minutes
Kōsuke has been trying hard to please me.
When I glare at him he deliberately blinks his eyes.
And his nose is black, I don't know why.
It may be that my anger comes
from my innate hatred of labor
and the fact that I haven't been feeling well since I came to the village;
because I don't know what to do about it,
now that Kōsuke has accepted the electric company's offer
and schemed a project like this,
I pour it all on him
the way supersaturated vapor
with tiny dust particles for a base
turns into rain.
Come to think of it,
the electric poles are not that unnecessary.
In fact, when I first came here
I wondered why the hell
they didn't have a single lamp.
Anyway, it isn't as easy as you might think
to glare at someone
when the wind is this cold
and the blue pungent smoke from Kōsuke's fire
hits me right in the face.
Two bottles of sake and five pieces of bean curd.
Kyūji, who lives near the woods,
brought the plates, soy sauce, and chopsticks.
The birches let their yellow leaves fly about,

the cedars drop brown needles.
Of the six linemen sent by the company
only one remains, like a hostage,
trying to get warm from the blue smoke.
Kōsuke didn't tell the others anything,
even the foreman, as they left,
but captured this one lingering, left behind,
like a specimen,
to give the appearance of 'thanking the linemen.'
As he tries hard to stir up the fire
and speaks words of thanks to him,
the lineman squats, ill at ease,
his dirty white hair straggling down
from his red-banded cap,
his Adam's apple risen to an unusual height.
The wind blows, blows from the west,
the cedars shake, red leaves of birches fall noisily.
Well, anyway, I'll join them.
But I will accept neither sake nor bean curd.
I will simply warm my hands over the fire
and glare at Kōsuke as fiercely as I can.
Then when I'm done I'll leave at once.

undated

■□ "A horse"

A horse
carefully wearing a load of rice
comes, with all its strength,
crossing a gleaming, shallow river in a blizzard.
The man as well
carrying on his back the wood of about ten pine trees
comes trudging, looking down.
From Horse Head to Table
the mountains make a row of white,
grass patches, woods and all.
Above, the sky pale, clear,
blows down, head-on,
a dry cold wind
which might be called a freezing sirocco,
and one is tempted to feel
the pale-gleaming sky is one's enemy.
Carrying an umbrella-shaped wood on his back,
thinking, A harvest of sixty loads instead of fifty
wouldn't make life a lot easier,
he comes quietly across the blizzard,
a resigned smile
on his lips shaped like lotus petals.
The horse, hair all splattered,
drenched with sweat,
plods on, blown by the blizzard.

undated

■◻ "In the leaden moonlight"

In the leaden moonlight
the enormous pine branches
lying here and there on the ground
might be mistaken for green rhinoceroses.
The recent sleet scraped
and thrashed them down
from the large treetops above.
The enormous shadows of the pine rows
and the moon-white net covering the grassland—
over there on the frozen riverbed
a naked baby was found abandoned.
From the cliff-top village
a suspect was led off,
the people petitioned—
that seems long ago.
Exactly a month later
before the frozen February daybreak
a woman crying wildly
calling a name
ran down the cliff to the river.
It must be the mother, pulled by the baby
to the river, I thought,
jumped out of bed and opened the door.
Then I heard a man catch up
and come back, soothing her.
The woman sobbed as she came
through the frozen mulberry field.

That much I could tell.
Then silence.
That seems even earlier.
Now the snow has all but vanished.
The river, gray as the sky,
glides south silently.
In the east, at Gorin Pass, curled winds
and syrupy clouds about to burst into tears
overhang, their hems vague, curled.
On this side, just above the dark river
plovers move along upstream.
How many times were you born? How many times frozen to death?
so they seem to sing.
Upstream, a haze white as wax,
and mountain forms are invisible.
From beneath the vague red light of town
the sound of a dog frantically barking—
the winds roar through the pines
again in cold broken rhythm.

undated

■▭ "Since the doctor is still young"

Since the doctor is still young,
they say he doesn't mind jumping out of bed at night,
discounts drugs for them, and doesn't do
complicated things like injections
or anything that desecrates nature too much.
I think that's why they like him.
By the time this doctor finally comes to feel
just as the villagers do,
and works as an integral part,
he'll have fallen behind in new techniques
and at the lecture of the county doctor's society
he'll curl up small, a perpetual listener.
Such is the effect of this sunlight,
water, and the transparent air.
Every time I pass here by train,
I try to imagine what kind of person he is.
Because, presiding over this beautiful hospital,
he has a face like a chameleon,
I feel very sorry for him.
Four or five persons have bowed.
Now the doctor quietly returns the bow.

undated

■□ Rest

On the ground cedar and zelkova roots
entangling, robbing each other
stand out like terrifying veins
from the grass and moss of this lean soil,
in the sky, clouds silently flowing east,
~~the cedar top withered,~~
the zelkova tip looking as if
it lives on snatches it takes from the wind
      . . . sometimes the cedar withers the zelkova
         sometimes the zelkova withers the cedar . . .
            (Harvest the rice, eat the rice, what for?
            Eat the rice, harvest the rice, what for?)
The technician shouts over there,
the trees, blurring, look half-melted in the sky,
and again, suffocating, the blue rice stalks.

undated

■□ Pneumonia

How come this grassblue, dark
enormous room is my lungs?
In it, jaundiced elementary schoolteachers
have been carrying on a grudgy conference for four hours already.
The pump, the pump's rackety,
arms and legs, I don't even know where they are.
None of these things seem mine any longer.
Except it's me who manages to think like this.
Damn it! Thinking's just thinking.
How the hell do you know it's you?
Then do you mean I don't exist. . . .
Oh shit! Don't start that now

undated

■□ Pictures of the Floating World

Glue and a small amount of alum
     . . . oh, network of billions of such
          microscopic delicate precise dots . . .
connect the snow-white tapa fibers
and form a fragile rectangular membrane
which increases or decreases sensitively with the humidity,
and breathes subtly, subtly with the temperature
     there
     etched suggestively are
     snow-fleshed or ivory-colored half-nude statues
     dyed lovingly are
     the nine monochromes
     as the light shifts
     they collapse feebly and fade
Look at these cheeks from a time long past
which now brim with insoluble smiles,
now transfuse too soluble passions
up to the slender eyes.
In the square brown-tiled room,
on the walls above the brown rug,
they hung like windows peering into the enormous
four-dimensional orbits.
The refined ladies and gentlemen of the Kingdom of Japan
endowed with religious beliefs of high grace and elegance
and with hereditary taste
stroll modestly oh so modestly
in each of the small paper spaces

none exceeding twelve square decimeters.
They purify, in that distant time and space,
the flames which too gentle models of lust
incite in their hearts,
and come and go lightly, eyebrows nobly raised.
They close the gap of time and space
and return in an instant to the paper
where, breathing the fragrance of old desires,
they pass by, absentminded, lightfooted.

There, the apple-green rich grassland,
the full water reflecting the thinly clouded sky,
the red torii shining small in the distance,
and the rows of decorative chrysocolla cedars.

Creators of the everlasting divine nation
Greatest authors of children's stories told visually

In the heavy, stagnant air
the wind is wearying,
and the woman, too sensual,
standing on the hill top, throws one, two, three
porcelain cups, which leave slight ripples
upon the viscid yellow waves.
And here, each ripple
is a great event.
In response appears
a white cloud, dazzling for the first time
and moves around the yellow hill
dotted with tiny pines.

Designer of a different atmosphere
and an innocent setting
In the autumn
they too thresh grain and cereal
and pull the clappers,
but with them the freezing point is fifty Fahrenheit,
the snow is cotton stacked up by the wind,
and when it piles up on wavy willows
it must do so by quite a different gravity.
In the summer, the rain does fall
from the black sky;
yet their leaf boats are moved
not so much by the wind as by their curiosity.
The water lilies are all of the kind called Lotus
and when they open, they make the evening air
tremble like a drum.

Such childhood soon turns
into burning, dazzling youth,
and the eyes loaded with rich love dance
and the quiet bones and muscles squeak.

Red fireworks, the water gleaming in the distance,
red lips inviting as,
say, raw tuna,
and around their eyes
a faint white of shyness
which may be on a wind's shadow
or may be what the paper has exuded.
Wanton eyebrows shaven blue.

Beneath the sharp second-day moon
their eyes, tired and dimmed,
reflect the gray roofs of the town.

The wind descends from the black sky,
the willow sways,
and lust flickers after the wind.

15 June 1928

Talking with Your Eyes

It's no use.
It won't stop.
See, it's bubbling up.
Since last night I haven't slept,
and the blood keeps coming out.
Everything I see around me is blue and quiet.
I feel I won't last long.
But what a fine wind.
Because it's almost daybreak,
it rises and swells from the blue sky,
the beautiful wind coming toward us,
setting young maple shoots and hair-like flowers
into the wavy motion of autumn grass.
Even the mats of nettle with burn scars look blue.
Perhaps you're on the way back from a doctors' convention,
wearing a frock coat like that,
and so sincere in trying to cure me.
So even if I die I'll make no complaint.
I'm bleeding, but I feel relaxed and all right,
because, I suppose, my soul has half left my body.
Anyway, because of the blood
I can't tell you that.
To your eyes I must be a horrible sight,
but my eyes see only
the beautiful blue sky
and the transparent wind.

1928/1929

◼▭ October 20th

Midnight, I wake with a start
and listen. Downstairs, on the west side,
ah, the child coughs and cries,
again coughs and cries.
In the intervals I hear her mother try
softly to persuade, try to soothe her.
Their room is cold.
During the day no sun shines in,
during the night, drafts come in through the floor boards.
In December, the third year of Shōwa,
when I had acute pneumonia in that room,
the child's father and mother, who were newly married,
gave me this large sunny room
and moved down there, a dark room
where I had lain for four months.
In February, she was born there.
For a girl she had a brave heart,
stumbling or falling she would not cry.
Last year, when I finally recovered
and began growing morning-glories and chrysanthemums,
she watered them,
she sometimes cut off the stalks with buds.
Toward the end of this past September I fell ill again in Tokyo.
I expected to die there,
but when again my parents' love helped me to return,
she welcomed me, smiling by the gate,
and then from the staircase
shouted at the top of her voice,

You've been gone a long time!
Now because of her fever, panting,
she can't control herself;
though one night she said, *Can't help it*,
and slept well,
tonight she just coughs and cries.
Mahābrahmadevaloka,
I am disturbed tonight in spite of myself
and humbly plead with you:
Though she is only three years old,
she already stands upright, joins her hands,
and recites the opening of the Lotus Sutra.
No matter what her sins in a former life,
may her illness, her pain,
be transferred to me.

1931

■◻ November 3rd

neither yielding to rain
nor yielding to wind
yielding neither to
snow nor to summer heat
    with a stout body
                like that
without greed
never getting angry
always smiling quiet-
                    ly
eating one and a half pints of brown rice
  and bean paste and a bit of
                        vegetables a day
in everything
not taking oneself
                into account
                looking listening understanding well
and not forgetting
living in the shadow of pine trees in a field
  in a small
        hut thatched with miscanthus
if in the east there's a
            sick child
going and nursing
                him
if in the west there's a tired mother
going and carrying

for her
bundles of rice
if in the south
there's someone
dying

going
and saying
you don't have to be
afraid
if in the north
there's a quarrel
or a lawsuit
saying it's not worth it
stop it
in a drought
shedding tears
in a cold summer
pacing back and forth   lost
called
a good-for-nothing
by everyone
neither praised
nor thought a pain
someone
like that
is what I want
to be

1931

Two Tanka

(Last Poems)

Within these ten square miles: is this in Hinuki alone?
The rice ripe and for three festival days
        the whole sky clear

———

Because of an illness, crumbling,
        this life—
if I could give it for ripening rice
        how glad I would be

20 September 1933

THREE STORIES

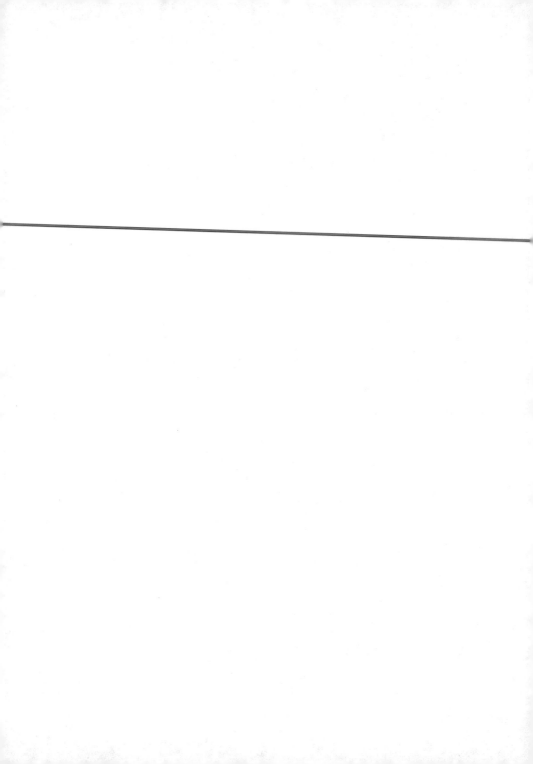

The Nighthawk Star

The nighthawk is a truly ugly bird.

His face is mottled as if bean-paste was smeared on it in spots, and his flat beak slits open from ear to ear.

His feet are as feeble as a very old man's, and he can't walk even a yard.

The other birds used to feel disgusted just looking at the nighthawk's face.

The lark, for example, isn't too beautiful a bird himself. But he felt he was far superior to the nighthawk, so that when he ran into him in the evenings he would deliberately close his eyes in visible disgust and look away. Smaller chatty birds would speak ill of him right to his face.

"Humph. He's trotted out again. Look at him. He's a real embarrassment among us birds."

"Right. See that. Such a huge mouth he has. I bet he's a relative of the frog or something."

That's the way they talked. Yes, if he had been a regular hawk, not a nighthawk, these half-baked little birds would have trembled at the mere mention of his name, turned pale, shriveled up, and hidden themselves behind the leaves. But the nighthawk wasn't the hawk's brother or relative. He was, rather, a big brother of that beautiful kingfisher, and the gem of all birds, the hummingbird. The hummingbird ate honey from flowers, the kingfisher ate fish, and the nighthawk ate winged insects. One reason the weakest birds weren't afraid of the nighthawk was that he had neither sharp claws nor a sharp beak.

You may wonder why he had the word "hawk" in his name. Well, that was because, for one thing, he had exceedingly powerful wings and when he cut through the wind he looked indeed like a hawk and, for another, his calls were sharp and somehow reminded you of a hawk. The hawk, the real one, didn't like this at all and was always worried about it. Every time he saw the nighthawk, he would raise his massive shoulders and tell him to change his name or else.

One evening, the hawk finally came to visit the nighthawk at his home.

"Hey, are you there?" the hawk said. "You haven't changed your name yet? Jeez, you have no sense of shame, do you. Do I need to tell you that there's a vast difference between you and me in dignity? Me, for example, I fly endlessly through the blue sky. You, on the other hand, don't come out unless it's a cloudy, murky day or at night.

"Then, too, look at my damned good beak," the hawk went on. "And compare that with the one you've got."

"Mr. Hawk, I can't change my name," the nighthawk replied. "I didn't give this name to myself. God gave it to me."

"No, sir," the hawk said. "With my name you might mention God and things, but your name—well, you just borrowed it from Night and me. Give me back my part of it. Right now."

"Mr. Hawk, I can't."

"You can," the hawk said. "I'll give you a good name. It's Ichizō. Ichizō. Good name, isn't it?

"Well now," the hawk continued, "when you change your name, you must make a formal announcement. To do that, you hang from your neck a plaque with the name 'Ichizō' written on it, visit everyone from house to house, formally announce your name-change by saying, 'From henceforth my name will be Ichizō,' and bow."

"I can't possibly do anything like that," the nighthawk protested.

"Yes, sir, you can," the hawk insisted. "Do exactly that. If you haven't done that by the morning of the day after tomorrow, I will tear you apart and kill you. Remember that: I will tear you apart and kill you. The day after tomorrow, early in the morning, I will visit every single one of the birds and ask if you have come to make the announcement. If even a single bird says you haven't, that will be the end of it for you. Understand?"

"That's too much, I just can't do that," the nighthawk said. "I'd rather die than do such a thing. You better kill me now, if that's what you want."

"Well, think it over. Ichizō isn't too bad a name." The hawk spread his large wings and flew away toward his nest.

The nighthawk closed his eyes and thought:

"Why is it that everyone is so put off by me? I know my face looks as if somebody put bean-paste on it, and my mouth slits from ear to ear. Still, I haven't done anything wrong in the past. When a baby white-eye fell from his nest, I helped him back up. But at the nest his mother took him from me as if I had kidnapped him. And how terribly she laughed at me! Now comes this Ichizō thing, I'm supposed to hang a plaque from my neck. All this is so painful."

Outside it was already darkening. The nighthawk flew out of his nest. The clouds gleamed meanly, hanging low. The nighthawk went up close to the clouds and flew about noiselessly in the sky.

Then he suddenly opened his mouth wide, spread his wings straight, and streaked across the sky downward like an arrow. Small winged insects flew into his throat one after another. Just before his body touched the ground, he made a swift turn and flew up into the sky again.

By then the clouds had turned gray, and a mountain fire beyond looked terribly red.

When the nighthawk flew with all his might, the sky looked as if cut in two. One beetle flew into his throat and struggled badly. He was able to swallow it soon, but he felt a chill run through him.

The clouds had turned totally black except some parts toward the east which reflected the red of the mountain fire and looked frightening. Feeling something stuck in his throat, the nighthawk climbed into the sky again.

Another beetle flew into his throat. This one scratched his throat as it thrashed about. The nighthawk tried to force it down, but suddenly his heart gave a thump. He began to weep loudly. As he wept, he flew round and round through the sky.

"Ah, I kill so many beetles and winged insects every night," the night-hawk thought. "And now the hawk is going to kill me. That's what gives me so much pain. Yes, it's so painful! I will no longer eat insects, and starve to death. No, before then, the hawk will kill me. No, no, before then I will fly away far beyond the distant, distant sky!"

The mountain fire slowly spread like water, and the clouds, too, appeared to be burning red.

The nighthawk flew straight to the nest of his kid brother, the kingfisher. The beautiful kingfisher had just awakened and was watching the mountain fire. As the nighthawk flew down, the kingfisher said:

"Good evening, brother. Is there anything I can do for you?"

"No, nothing," the nighthawk said. "I am going away to a distant place, and wanted to say goodbye to you."

"No, don't go, brother," said the kingfisher. "Our other brother, the hum-mingbird, already lives far away. If you went, I'd become totally alone."

"Well, I can't help it. Please don't say anything more now. Here's one thing I might say to you: Don't catch fish you don't need, don't catch them for the fun of it. OK? Now, goodbye."

"What's the matter with you, brother? Wait a minute!"

"No, my staying here longer won't make any difference. If you meet the hummingbird, give my regards, will you? Goodbye. I won't see you again. Goodbye."

Weeping, the nighthawk returned to his home. The short summer night was already ending.

The leaves of fern, absorbing the daybreak dew, swayed blue, cold. The nighthawk gave a few sharp calls. He then put his nest in neat order, preened his feathers thoroughly, and flew out again.

The mists cleared. Just then the sun rose in the east. Its blinding light al-most made the nighthawk stagger, but he flew toward it like an arrow.

"Mr. Sun, Mr. Sun," he called out. "Please accept me. I will not mind burning to death. I have an ugly body, but when I burn even I may give out a small amount of light. Please accept me."

The nighthawk flew and flew, but the sun did not grow near. Instead, becoming gradually smaller and more distant, the sun said:

"I see, you are the nighthawk. I understand that it is all very painful for you. But fly in the sky tonight and ask the star. You are not a daytime bird after all."

The nighthawk thought he had bowed to the sun once, but he suddenly felt himself stagger, and finally he fell down to the grass in the field. Afterward it was as if he was dreaming dreams. Now his body rose through the stars, red and yellow; now it was blown away endlessly in the wind; now it was as if the hawk came and grabbed it.

Something cold dropped on his face. The nighthawk opened his eyes. It was a dewdrop from a leaf of young pampas grass. It was already night, and the sky was dark-blue, with stars twinkling all across its face. The nighthawk flew up into the sky. Tonight, too, the mountain fire was burning red. The nighthawk made a single flight amid the faint reflections of the fire and the cold star light. He made another. Then with some determination he flew straight toward that beautiful Orion to the west, calling out:

"Mr. Orion, Mr. Orion, Pale-blue Star to the West. Please accept me. I will not mind burning to death."

Orion, continuing to sing his stirring, manly song, didn't even try to respond to the nighthawk. The nighthawk, on the brink of tears, tottered in midair, fell a little, but pulled himself back, and flew around once more. He then headed straight toward the Great Dog to the south, calling out:

"Mr. Dog, Blue Star to the South. Please accept me. I will not mind burning to death."

Busily, beautifully twinkling blue, purple, and yellow, the Great Dog turned to him and barked:

"Don't be a fool. What do you think you are anyway? You are a mere bird.

For you to reach here it would take billions and billions of years." He then looked away.

Disappointed, the nighthawk tottered down, but he circled around twice more. Then, determined once again, he headed straight toward the Great Bear to the north, calling out:

"Mr. Bear, Blue Star to the North, please accept me."

The Great Bear said quietly:

"Don't think such useless things. Go back and cool your head a little. When you are hot-headed like that, the best cure is to jump into the sea with icebergs floating in it, or jump into a glass with ice cubes floating in it."

Disappointed, the nighthawk tottered down, but he flew around the sky four more times. And once again he called out—this time to the Eagle to the east on the other side of the Milky Way that had just risen:

"White Star to the East, please accept me. I will not mind burning to death."

The Eagle said grandly:

"No, no, what's all this nonsensical talk! To become a star, you've got to have an appropriate social status. You must also have a good deal of money."

Hearing this, the nighthawk lost all his energy, and with his wings closed, fell toward the earth. But just before his feeble feet touched the ground, he suddenly flew up into the sky like a beacon. When he reached mid-sky, he shook his body once and bristled, just as an eagle does when he readies himself to attack a bear.

Then the nighthawk gave sharp, sharp calls. He sounded exactly like a hawk. The birds that were asleep in the fields and in the forests woke up and, trembling with fear, suspiciously looked up at the starry sky.

The nighthawk continued to climb up into the sky endlessly, endlessly. The mountain fire now looked no larger than a lighted cigarette stub. He climbed and climbed.

It was so cold that his breath froze on his chest. As the air grew thinner and thinner, he had to beat his wings harder, much harder.

Even so, the sizes of the stars had not changed at all. The nighthawk began to breathe like a bellows. The cold and the frost stabbed him like swords. His wings became numb. He looked up at the sky once again with his teary eyes. And yes, that was the end of the nighthawk. He no longer knew whether he was falling or climbing, was upside down or turned upward. But he felt peaceful. His large beak, stained with blood, was crooked sideways, but I can tell you that he certainly had a faint smile on his face.

After some while the nighthawk opened his eyes clearly. And he saw that his body had turned into a beautiful blue ball of phosphorescent fire and was quietly burning.

Right next to him was the Cassiopeia. Right behind him was the pale-blue stream of light of the Milky Way.

And the nighthawk star continued to burn. It went on burning on and on. It still does.

The Ground God and the Fox

1

At the northern end of the Lone Tree Field, there was a small mound covered with foxtail. In the middle of the mound stood a beautiful birch tree.

She was not tall, but her trunk shone black as if polished, and her branches stretched out beautifully. In May, she put on white flowers like puffs of cloud, and in autumn she scattered golden and red leaves.

The migrating cuckoos and shrikes, and other small birds like wrens and white-eyes, all came to stay in her branches. But when birds like young hawks came there, the smaller ones spotted them far off and would not come near.

The birch tree had two friends. One was the ground god who lived in a muddy swamp about five hundred steps away, the other a brown fox who always came from the south of the field. If she had to make the choice, the birch would have said she liked the fox better. Though he was called a god, the ground god was quite violent, and his hair looked like a bundle of tattered cotton threads, his eyes were bloodshot, and what he wore most resembled a large piece of kelp. Besides, he always tramped about barefoot, his toenails black and long. The fox, on the other hand, looked very elegant and seldom did things that would anger or annoy people.

Still, if you compared the two of them carefully, you might have found the ground god honest and the fox a little dishonest.

2

It was a night in early summer. The birch wore an abundance of fresh, soft leaves and her fragrance filled the air. In the sky, the Milky Way had already

228

laid out its white self, and the stars were trembling and swaying, turning on and off.

The fox came to visit with a book of poetry. He was wearing a dark-blue jacket just made, and his red leather shoes clicked rhythmically as he walked.

"Miss Birch, it's such a quiet night, isn't it?" the fox said.

"Yes, Mr. Fox," the birch replied softly.

"Do you see Scorpius crawling over there? In the old days, the Chinese used to call that big red star 'Fire.'"

"Don't they also call Mars 'the Fire Star'?"

"Ah, but that's different. You see," the fox said, "Mars is a planet, but that red one is a real star."

"What's the difference between a planet and a star?" asked the birch.

"A planet doesn't shine by itself. That is," said the fox, "a planet looks as if it shines, but actually it gets light from other sources. A star shines by itself. So, you see, the sun is a star. The sun is so large and dazzling, but I imagine that if you looked at it from an immense distance, it would look as small as other stars."

"You say the sun is a star?" said the birch, surprised. "It means there are a lot of suns in the sky—no, I mean a lot of stars—that's odd, too. I suppose they're suns, aren't they?"

"Yes," the fox laughed expansively.

"I wonder why there are red stars, yellow stars, and green stars," she mused aloud.

The fox laughed expansively again and crossed his arms high upon his chest. The book of poetry he held danced precariously at his fingertips, but it didn't quite fall.

"You wonder why there are olive stars and blue stars?" he began. "You see, in the beginning all the stars were some kind of vague, cloudlike stuff. There's plenty of such stuff in the sky even now. It's in Andromeda, Orion, and Canis Major. The stuff in Canis Major is spiral. Some of it is called Ring Nebula. Ring Nebula is also called Fish-Mouth Nebula because it's shaped like the mouth of a fish. Anyway, there's quite a number of such formations in the sky."

"How I want to see one!" the birch said. "A star shaped like the mouth of a fish—it must be very good!"

"It really is," said the fox. "I actually saw some at the observatory at Mizusawa."

"Do you think I can see some myself?"

"I will give you a chance," said the fox. "In fact, I have just ordered a telescope from Zeiss & Co. in Germany. I expect to get it before next spring. As soon as I get it, I'll show some to you."

That was not what he had meant to say. Having said it, the fox thought to himself:

Ah, I lied again to my only friend. I'm no good at all. I didn't do it out of malicious intentions, though. I just wanted to please her. I'll tell her all the truth when the time comes.

Such was the thought the fox had for a while in silence. Not knowing any such thing, the birch said happily:

"I'm so glad to hear that. You are always so kind."

"I'd do any other thing for you," said the fox, rather crestfallen. "Would you like to look at this book of poems? It's by Heine. They're translations, but I think they're pretty good."

"Oh, my. May I borrow it?" the birch asked.

"You certainly may. Take your time," said the fox. "Now I must go. Come to think of it, I seem to have forgotten to say something."

"About different colors of the stars."

"You're right. If you'll excuse me, however, I'll tell you about it next time. I shouldn't stay too long with you."

"No, I don't mind."

"I'll come again," said the fox. "Good night. You may keep the book. Good night."

The fox hurried away. The birch, letting her leaves rustle in the south wind that had just begun to blow, picked up the book of poetry the fox had left, and turned the pages in the faint light from the Milky Way and the other stars that filled the whole sky. The Heine book was filled with "Lorelei" and other beautiful poems. She read all through the night, except when she dozed off for a moment about three in the morning as Taurus began to rise in the east.

Day broke. The sun rose. Grass glittered with dew, and flowers bloomed with all their might.

From the northeast, bathed in the sun, his body looking as if he had smeared molten copper all over it, the ground god came slowly, slowly. His arms folded as if immersed in some discriminating thoughts, he came slowly, slowly.

When she saw him, the birch felt a little worried. Even so, making her blue leaves glisten, she turned toward him. Her shadow falling on the grass below swayed, twinkling, twinkling.

"Good morning, Miss Birch," the ground god said as he quietly stopped in front of her.

"Good morning, Mr. Ground God," replied the birch.

"You know, once you start thinking, it's difficult to understand lots of things," the ground god said. "In fact, there are a great many things I don't understand."

"My, what sort of things?" the birch asked.

"For example, grasses. Why are they so green, coming out of black earth as they do? They even have yellow or white flowers. I don't understand that at all."

"That, I should imagine," the birch suggested, "is because their seeds have green and white in them."

"Yes. I suppose that's the right answer, but I still don't understand," the ground god persisted. "Take mushrooms in the fall. They don't even have seeds, they just come out of the earth. And yet, some of them are red, some of them yellow. I really don't understand."

"Why don't you ask Mr. Fox?" said the birch rather carelessly. She was still somewhat entranced about the conversation on stars that she'd had with the fox the previous night.

The ground god's reaction was immediate. He turned pale, he clenched his fists. "Did you say 'fox'? What did a mere fox have to say?"

"He didn't say anything," the birch said, her voice already trembling. "I just thought he might know."

"Do you mean to suggest that a god learn from a fox? Damn it!" said the ground god.

The birch, now really frightened, trembled, quivered. The ground god stomped around, gnashing his teeth, his arms crossed high on his chest. The shadow he cast lay coal-black on the grass, and the terrified grass too trembled.

"The fox does nothing but harm to the world," the ground god declared. "Not a single word he utters is true. He is cowardly, timid, and extremely jealous. Besides, he's just a beast."

"The festival in your honor is very near, isn't it?" said the birch, as she finally regained her composure.

"It is," the ground god said. He softened a little. "Today is the third of May, which means six more days." He pondered a while. Then angry again, he began to shout. "But human beings are insufferable. They don't even bother to bring offerings any more." He ground his teeth. "I swear here and now that I will drag into the bottom of the mud the first man I see step in my territory."

The birch had meant to soothe the god with her words, but he only grew more angry. Now utterly lost, she only let her leaves imperceptibly quiver in the wind. The ground god wandered around, almost aflame in the sun, his arms crossed high on his chest, grinding his teeth terribly. It was obvious that

232

the more he thought, the more annoyed, the more frustrated he became. Eventually, he couldn't take it any more. Half barking, half groaning, he suddenly stomped back toward his valley.

3

The ground god lived in a cold swamp the size of a small racetrack where there was only moss, withered grass, short reeds, and in a few spots some thistles and stumpy, extremely twisted boxtrees. The water was dank, and where iron rust bubbled up it looked slimy and a little scary too. On a small islandlike spot in the swamp stood a shrine built for the ground god. It was about six feet high and made with logs.

The ground god came back to the island and scratched his black scrawny legs as he lay lazily by the shrine. A few moments later, he saw a bird sweep straight across the sky overhead. He sat up and hissed. The bird was shocked. He fluttered as if about to drop. He flew on, but he fell gradually toward the earth, as if his wings and all were paralyzed.

The ground god smiled slightly and rose to his feet. But then, he happened to look toward the mound where the birch tree stood. Instantly, he turned pale, and his whole body stiffened. As if to show his great frustration, he tore at the tattered bundle of his hair.

Then he saw a woodcutter coming from the south of the valley. The woodcutter headed toward the Triple Forest Mountain, apparently to make some money, and walked in large strides along the narrow path by the swamp. Every now and then, he turned a worried look toward the shrine. Obviously he knew about the ground god. But he could not see him because the ground god was invisible to man.

The ground god flushed red with joy when he saw the woodcutter. He thrust his right arm toward him, and gripping with his left hand the wrist of his right arm, pulled it slowly toward himself. Then an odd thing happened: the woodcutter began to lose his way and step into the swamp. Alarmed, he quickened his pace. He turned pale and began to pant. The ground god then slowly drew a circle in the air with his right fist. The woodcutter began to walk in a circle. He grew more alarmed, but the harder he tried to get out of the swamp, the more difficult it became to get away from the spot where he circled round and round. He began to whimper. And finally he threw up his arms and started to run.

The ground god watched all this, lying on the ground grinning with pleasure, until the woodcutter, worked up and exhausted, fell flat on his face in the water. The ground god stood up slowly, waded through the muddy water to the man, picked him up, and threw him out into the field. As he dropped with a thud on the grass, the woodcutter groaned and moved a little, but did not come to.

The ground god laughed loudly. The sound of his laughter turned into a strange wave and went up toward the sky. Then, it bounced back in midair and fell with a thump near the birch tree. She turned pale and, almost invisibly blue in the sunlight, quivered busily, busily.

The ground god brooded, tearing at his hair with both hands as if in despair. I'm in such a terrible mood, first, because of the fox. No, it's not so much because of the fox as because of the birch. It's because of the fox and the birch. But I'm not angry with the birch. It's so painful because I'm not angry with her. If I didn't care for the birch, I couldn't care less about the fox. I'm contemptible, but at least I'm a god. How humiliating that a god should have to worry about a mere fox! But I worry about him, and there's nothing I can do about it. Forget about the birch, I tell myself, but I can't, try as I may. This morning, when she turned pale and trembled, how fine she was! I can't forget her. Only because of this frustration I played such a nasty trick on the poor man. One will do almost anything in frustration!

The ground god, feeling helpless, kicked and struggled. A hawk swept across the sky, but this time the ground god just watched it in silence.

Far in the distance, cavalry appeared to be engaged in a maneuver; the popping noise of their rifle shots, like sesame seeds being broiled, reached the swamp. From the sky, blue light poured into the field. Perhaps because he swallowed some of it, the woodcutter came to in the grass. He sat up timidly, and looked around closely. Then he jumped to his feet and darted off toward the Triple Forest Mountain.

The ground god laughed loudly. Again, his laughter rose in the sky, and again it turned back in midair and fell with a thump near the birch tree. Her leaves turned pale and almost invisibly quivered.

The ground god walked back and forth, back and forth, in front of his shrine. When finally he calmed down, he melted noiselessly into it.

4

It was a foggy night in August. The ground god, feeling indescribably lonely and frustrated, sauntered out of his shrine. Before he knew it, he was walking in the direction of the birch tree. The truth was, though he didn't know why, his heart would give a thump each time he thought of her. And he would feel helpless. Recently, though, his feelings had changed a lot, and for the better. As much as he could, he tried not to think about the fox, about the birch. Still, his thoughts kept returning to them. The least I can say about myself is that I'm a god, aren't I? he asked himself every day. What value does a single birch tree have for me? Yet, he was so sad, and he didn't know what to do about it. Worse, any passing thought of the fox gave him the sort of pain that burning would have.

Musing about such things, the ground god came gradually near the birch tree. When finally he noticed where he was going, his heart started to dance oddly. And it occurred to him that he had not seen her for a long time. It's possible that she's waiting for me, he thought. I sense that she is. If she is, I should be very sorry for her. The thought encouraged him and he began to clomp over the grass in large strides, joyfully, toward the birch. But soon his powerful strides faltered and he stopped, bathed in blue sorrow from his head down. He had recognized the fox with the birch. In the depth of the night, through the fog stagnant in the hazy moonlight, the fox's voice reached him:

"Yes, of course, that goes without saying," the fox was exclaiming. "A thing can't be beautiful simply because it follows mechanically the law of symmetry. If there's beauty in that, it's a dead beauty."

"You are so right, Mr. Fox," the ground god heard the birch's quiet voice respond.

"True beauty," the fox went on, "is not anything like such a rigid, fossilized model. What is desirable is keeping the spirit of symmetry rather than following its law exactly."

"Oh, I agree with you so," again the ground god heard the birch's gentle voice say. This time he felt as if his whole body was burnt in rosy flames. He became short of breath, he couldn't take it any more. What makes me feel so helplessly sad? It's just a brief conversation in the field between a birch tree and a fox. If something like that disturbs you, how can you call yourself a god? The ground god reproached himself.

"In fact, any book on aesthetics discusses that much," the fox continued.

"You must have many books on aesthetics," said the birch.

"Not so many, but I think I have most of the books in Japanese, English, and German. There are some new ones in Italian, but I don't have them yet."

"How splendid your study must look!"

"Well, things are scattered all over. You see, I use it as my lab, too. So, a microscope in one corner, a pile of the London *Times* in another, a marble bust of Caesar lying on the floor—actually it's really cluttered and untidy."

"That's splendid, splendid," said the birch. To that, the fox gave a short snort, which sounded at once humble and boastful. Silence followed.

The ground god could no longer contain himself. What the fox said proved unmistakably that the fox was much more intelligent than he. How many times had he tried to persuade himself that he was a god, if nothing else? Now, that persuasion would not work. This is all so painful, painful! Should I jump out and tear the fox to shreds? No, no, I mustn't even dream of such a thing, for what am I after all? A god lesser than a fox, that's what I am. The ground god writhed.

"Have you received the telescope you mentioned before?" the birch asked.

"I remember talking about that," answered the fox. "I'm sorry, but I haven't, not yet. The sea-lane to Europe is pretty congested lately. But as soon as I get it, I'll bring it right over and show it to you. Oh, you should see the rings around Saturn, for example. They are so beautiful."

The ground god suddenly shut his ears with his hands and started dashing toward the north. He didn't know what he might do next, and that terrified him.

He ran blindly. In the end, he ran out of breath and fell on the ground, at the foot of the Triple Forest Mountain.

The ground god rolled on the grass, tearing his hair. Then he wept loudly. The sound of his grief reached the sky and rumbled like an untimely thunder. He wept and wept, until he was exhausted. In the morning, he went back to his shrine, feeling rather disoriented.

5

Autumn came. The birch was still all green, but the foxtails around her already had golden ears, which glistened in the wind. In some places, there were lilies-of-the-valley, with ripened red seeds.

One transparent, golden day, the ground god felt unusually good. It was as if all those painful thoughts that had tormented him throughout the summer had turned indistinct but somehow admirable, and now hovered above his head like a halo. He felt that the nasty part of his character had mysteriously left him. Indeed, if the birch wants to talk with the fox, she should, the ground god decided. If both birch and fox enjoy talking with each other, there must be something really good in it. As he walked toward the birch tree, thinking that he would tell this to her, his heart was buoyant.

The birch tree saw all that from where she stood, but still she trembled worriedly.

"Good morning, Miss Birch," the ground god said casually, as he came near her. "It's such good weather, isn't it?"

"Good morning, Mr. Ground God. Yes, it is such good weather."

"You know, one cannot help being grateful to the sun," said the ground god. "It's red in spring, white in summer, and yellow in autumn. And as the autumn turns yellow, grapes turn purple. Indeed, one can only be grateful."

"You are right, Mr. Ground God," said the birch.

"I must tell you something, Miss Birch," the ground god said. "I feel extremely good today. I had a number of painful experiences to go through during the summer, but this morning I suddenly began to feel lighthearted."

The birch wanted to respond to this, but she couldn't. To her, the ground god's words seemed heavy with something.

"Now I feel I could give up my soul for anyone," the ground god went on. "If an earthworm has to die, I'd be glad to die for him." The ground god was looking into the distance, at the blue sky. His black eyes had a noble look.

The birch again wanted to respond, but could not. Something in his words weighed on her. She sighed.

It was then that the fox came. The fox turned pale, seeing the ground god, but he knew it was awkward to turn away.

"Good morning, Miss Birch," he said, trembling slightly, as he proceeded to where the birch tree stood. "This morning, I seem to see Mr. Ground God as well. How are you, Mr. Ground God?" He was in a brown raincoat and red leather shoes. He still wore a summer hat.

"Yes, I'm Ground God," said the ground god, feeling truly bright. "It's such good weather, isn't it?"

"It's rude of me to show up when you have a guest," the fox said to the birch, his face pale with jealousy. "This is the book I promised to bring over the other day. And one more thing. I'll be glad to show you the telescope some clear night. Goodbye."

The fox started to leave even before the birch finished saying thank you, without saying anything to the ground god. The birch suddenly turned pale and quivered delicately.

For a while, the ground god was watching, in a rather absentminded fashion, the fox going away. But as the fox's red leather shoes glistened in the grass, he woke up, and his brain reeled. Now he clearly saw the fox striding off, his shoulders squared in apparent defiance. The ground god felt anger seethe up. His face turned horribly black.

Always prattling about aesthetics and telescopes, damn it. Now I'll show him what I can do, he swore, suddenly in mad chase after the fox. The birch was alarmed, and all her branches shook violently. The fox felt it and looked back. The ground god was right after him, like a black hurricane. The fox turned blue as he started running, his mouth crooked.

To the ground god, it was as if all the grass around him had caught fire, white. Even the sky that had been shining blue turned into an empty black void where scarlet flames roared.

The ground god and the fox ran like thundering locomotives.

"I'm finished, I'm finished. Telescope, telescope, telescope," the fox thought in the corner of his head, running as in a dream.

Reaching a small red bald hill, the fox rushed half around it to get into a round hole at the bottom. He was half in the hole, his hind legs kicking up in the air, when the ground god crashed on him. The next moment, the fox was lying in the ground god's arms, his body twisted, his pointed mouth half smiling, his head rolling lifelessly.

The ground god threw him down on the ground and stomped on his squishy body four or five times.

Then, he jumped abruptly into the fox's hole. Inside, it was empty and dark. All he could see was neatly trodden clay. He came out, opening his mouth in a greatly distorted way, feeling a little odd. He fumbled in the pockets of the raincoat the dead fox wore. All he found were two brown ears of reed. The ground god, with his mouth still open, burst into tears, crying deafeningly aloud.

His tears fell like rain upon the fox, his hanging head looking even more lifeless, his face still faintly smiling.

The Bears of Nametoko

If it's about the bears of Nametoko, I can tell you a good story. Nametoko is a large mountain. From there the Fuchizawa River flows. Most days of the year, the mountain breathes in and out cold mists or clouds. The surrounding mountains also look like dark-blue sea cucumbers or monsters from the depths. Halfway up the mountain, the hollow mouth of a large cave gapes. The Fuchizawa River suddenly drops three hundred feet out of the cave, roaring down among clusters of cypress and maple.

Because no one walks the Nakasen Road nowadays, it is overgrown with winter heliotrope and knotweed, and it has fences put up to prevent cattle from wandering off to the mountain. But, if you rustle ahead about seven miles, you'll hear in the distance a sound like the wind passing over the mountaintop. There, if you look carefully in that direction, you'll see something white and thin—you can't tell what it is—moving down the mountain, pushing whiffs of smoke aside. That's Nametoko's Great Sky Fall. In the old days, they say, a whole jumble of bears lived near it. To tell the truth, I myself actually have never seen either Mt. Nametoko or the liver of a bear. All I have to tell is what I have heard or what I have imagined. I may be wrong in parts, but I must tell the story as I know it.

The bear livers from Mt. Nametoko are quite famous. They work for stomach ache, they heal wounds. The sign board at the entrance of the Lead Hot Spa, which says, We Carry Nametoko Bear Livers, has been hanging there since the olden days. So I'm certain that the bears still cross valleys, with their wet red tongues lolling, and their cubs wrestle and punch each other with their paws. The master of bear-hunting Fuchizawa Kojūrō used to hunt them one by one.

Kojūrō was a cross-eyed, dark-reddish bundle of muscles of a fellow, his girth almost the size of a small mortar, and his palm as thick and large as the illness-curing plaque of the Bishamon, the Listening God, at Kitajima. In summers, he wore his raincoat made of lime bark, put on leggings, and carried a hatchet only primitive people might use and a huge heavy musket slung over his shoulder, which looked as if it came straight from Portugal. So equipped, with his sturdy, yellow dog, he freely traversed the entire area, from Mt. Nametoko to the Shidoke Valley, from the Three-way to Sakkai, from the Badger Den Forest to the White Valley.

When you go up a valley stream where lots of trees grow, you feel as if you are going through a dark-blue tunnel, which sometimes suddenly opens up bright, all green and gold, or leads to sunrays scattered like flowers that have just bloomed. When walking up a place like that, Kojūrō never hurried, ponderous in his measured strides, as if in his own guest room. Always ahead of him was his dog. It would scurry by the bank, splash into the water, swim for dear life across a pool where the stagnant water is slimy and frightening, reach and climb up the rock on the other side, shake the water off, and, wrinkling its nose, wait for its master to catch up. And Kojūrō would come, his mouth warped a little, making stiff white screens of foam above his knees as he plied his legs like compasses. It's bad form to tell you everything at once, but the bears in and around Mt. Nametoko liked Kojūrō a lot.

For you see, when Kojūrō sploshed through the valley or walked the flat strip of shore covered with thistles, the bears watched him in silence, obviously amused, from high places, some holding on to a tree with both arms, some sitting on the cliff-top with knees held in their paws.

Indeed, the bears seemed to like even Kojūrō's dog.

Of course, they didn't much like having to confront Kojūrō face-to-face, with the dog attacking like a fireball, the hunter aiming his gun, eyes oddly glinting. At such a time, most bears would wave their hands and refuse to have something like that done to them.

But there are many kinds of bears. Some, especially the fierce-tempered ones, would rise to their feet with terrible roars and, almost trampling on his dog, charge toward Kojūrō, their arms thrust forward. But Kojūrō was always calm. He would plant himself against a tree and shoot at the white ring around the bear's neck. When that happened even the forest roared with the bear. Then the animal would fall on the ground with a thud and die, whimpering as darkish blood gushed out of the wound.

Then Kojūrō would put his gun against the tree, go up to the bear cautiously, and say:

"Bear, I didn't kill you because I hated you. This is my job and I've got to shoot you. I'd like to do some more innocent work, but I have no land, and they decided that the trees belong to the Authorities. Down there in the village, no one wants to deal with me. I hunt because I've got to. It's bad luck that you were born a bear, it's bad luck that I do business like this. Look, next time, don't be born a bear."

While Kojūrō spoke, his dog would sit by, completely dejected, its eyes narrowed. The dog had survived, alive and kicking, Kojūrō's fortieth summer, when his entire family came down with dysentery and his son and wife died.

After he spoke, Kojūrō would take out his well-honed knife and slit open the bear from the chin, through the breast, down to the belly. I hate what happens after that. Anyway, in the end, I know Kojūrō would put the blood-red liver of the bear in the wooden casket on his back, wash in the stream nearby the pelt whose hair formed knots with blood, roll it up, put it on his back, and start downstream, himself looking as inert as the pelt.

After a long time spent among bears, he came to think he understood their language. One early spring day before a single tree had turned green, Kojūrō went up with his dog far into the White Valley. In the evening, when he came to the hilltop leading down to Bakkai Dale, he decided to stay overnight at the bamboo-grass hut he had built the previous summer. But, quite unlike him, while he thought he'd been heading toward the hut, he realized he had come the wrong way. He turned down to the valley and started up again. Again it was the wrong way. He had to do this many more times before finding the half-crumbling hut. By that time, the dog was exhausted, and he himself was breathing through his mouth crooked sideways.

He remembered there was a spring a little downhill. It was on his way down that he saw to his surprise two bears, a mother bear and a cub, hardly a year old. In the soft six-day moonlight, they were gazing intently at the other side of the valley, their paws poised above their eyes just like people. To Kojūrō it seemed as if the two bears had haloes. As if nailed to the spot, he stopped, and watched. Then, he heard the cub say, like a spoiled kid:

"Mommy, I don't care what you say, that is snow. See, only this side of the valley is white. No matter what you say, that's snow, Mommy."

The mother bear kept looking intently. Finally she said, "That's not snow. It can't snow only there."

"So I say it hasn't melted yet," the cub replied.

"No, you're wrong," the mother said. "Just yesterday I passed there on my way to see thistle buds."

Kojūrō too looked intently in the same direction. The part of the slope where the blue moonlight seemed to flow was shining like silver armor. After a while, the cub said, "If it's not snow, it's frost. I'm sure of that."

Certainly we'll have frost tonight, Kojūrō thought to himself. See near the moon the Ram shivering blue? And the moon looks icy in the first place.

"I know what that is," the mother said. "That's the flowers of shepherd's purse."

"Oh sure," the cub responded quickly. "They *are* the flowers of shepherd's purse. I know what they look like."

"No, I don't think you have ever seen them."

"Yes I have. Remember I got some the other day?"

"No, they weren't shepherd's purse. What you had were the flowers of Indian beans."

"Oh they were?" replied the cub, pretending not to know.

Somehow, Kojūrō was deeply moved. Before going off very quietly, he glanced once again at the snow-white flowers on the other side of the valley and once more at the mother bear and the cub bathed peacefully in the moonlight. As he slowly backed away, he was fearful of his scent blowing in the direction of the bears. The fragrance of camphor trees and the moonlight suddenly penetrated the silence.

This same tough Kojūrō was a miserable and pitiful sight when he went down to the town to sell bear pelts and livers.

Near the middle of the town there was a large general store which carried things like baskets, sugar, whetstones, cigarettes with brand names like Golden Dragon and Chameleon, and even flytraps made of glass. Whenever Kojūrō crossed its threshold with a mountainous bundle of bear pelts on his back, the store seemed to say, "Here he comes again," with a thin-lipped sneer. The storemaster was in the room next to the store, installed grandly behind a large brass heater.

"Master, thank you again for buying from me the other day." Kojūrō, the true master in the mountains, began always with these words, after carefully putting his load of pelts next to him and politely placing his hands on the floorboard for greetings.

"Well, what is your business today?" The storemaster's response was always the same too.

"I brought a few more bear pelts."

"Bear pelts? The ones you brought last haven't sold yet. I don't think I want any more for a while."

"Master, please buy these," Kojūrō was already pleading. "I can give them to you very cheap."

"Cheap or not, I don't need them, that's all." The storemaster, calm and composed, would thereupon slap his pipe against his palm. And, routine though these words were, they always made Kojūrō frown worriedly.

There was good reason for that. Kojūrō could collect chestnuts in the mountains and grow some millet on the small patch of land behind his house. But he couldn't grow rice there and had no bean-paste. He needed money to buy rice, however small the amount, for his large household, his ninety-year-old mother and five children. Besides, unlike the village people who could grow hemp, Kojūrō couldn't grow anything with which to make cloth, though he could use wisteria fiber to make a few baskets.

After a while, Kojūrō would repeat in a voice now grown too husky: "Master, I plead with you. I don't mind how much. Please buy these." Then he would again bow deeply.

The storemaster wouldn't say a word but for a while would exhale smoke. Finally, trying to hide a happy snicker, he would say, "All right, leave them, then. Hey, Heisuke, give Kojūrō two yen, will you?"

Heisuke, the store clerk, would come out and place four large silver coins before Kojūrō. Kojūrō, now smiling happily, would accept them in both hands in extreme gratitude.

After that, the storemaster's mood would visibly improve.

"Well now, Okino, would you serve Kojūrō a drink?"

By that time, Kojūrō himself would be all happiness. The master would talk leisurely about various things. Kojūrō would be attentive and formal, telling him about the goings-on in the mountains. Soon, word would come from the kitchen that the drink was ready. Kojūrō would decline rather halfheartedly, only to be pulled into the kitchen after all. There, he would again bow politely.

Soon, a small black tray would be placed in front of him with a bottle of sake on it, along with tidbits like sliced salted salmon and squid. For a while Kojūrō would sit there formally, now licking the salted squid he picked up on his palm, now reverentially pouring the yellow sake into a small cup.

Prices were low then, but two yen for two bear pelts was too cheap, everybody thought.

Indeed, it was cheap, and Kojūrō himself knew it. Then why didn't he try to sell to other people instead of such a miserly storekeeper? Most people don't know the answer, except that in Japan people believe in what is called the "Fox Syndrome." The idea is, it's predetermined that the hunter will beat the fox, the rich merchant the hunter, and the cunning fox the merchant. In Kojūrō's case, he beat the bear, the storemaster beat Kojūrō, but as for the storemaster, since he lived in the middle of a town, the bear couldn't eat him up. However, such disgusting double-dealers as this storemaster will eventually disappear as the world makes progress.

It annoys me to no end that I've had to write, if only briefly, how this disgusting man, whose face I wouldn't even want to see, so easily gulled someone as remarkable as Kojūrō.

So, Kojūrō didn't hate the bears, though he killed them. One summer, though, something odd happened, as we will see.

When he had splashed along the valley and climbed on a rock, he saw right in front a large bear shinnying up a tree, its back rounded like a cat. Instantly, he turned his gun on the bear. The dog, delighted, was already running madly around the tree.

The bear on the tree seemed to ponder for a moment whether it should jump at Kojūrō or be shot in that position. Then, suddenly it let go of the tree and dropped with a thud on the ground. Kojūrō went up to the bear, his gun poised. The bear raised its arms and asked, "What do you want to kill me for?"

"All I want is your pelt and liver," Kojūrō said. "I know I can't get a good price for them in town, and I really feel sorry for you, but what can I do? But now that you've asked me that, I feel I should be eating acorns and chestnuts and, if I starve to death because of that, I shouldn't mind."

"Could you wait two years?" the bear said. "At my age I shouldn't mind dying either, but I have some work left to do. Two years should be enough. In two years I'll come and die in front of your house. Then you may take my pelt and liver."

The bear's offer gave the hunter a funny feeling. He lapsed into thought.

247

Meanwhile, the bear started to walk away slowly, all paws on the ground. Kojūrō did not move.

The bear walked away slowly, slowly, without once looking back, as if it knew Kojūrō would never shoot it from behind. When the bear's expansive, dark-reddish back gleamed in the sunlight that fell through the tree leaves above, Kojūrō gave a low moan in a helpless manner and started back along the valley.

It was exactly two years afterward. One morning, the wind was blowing so hard Kojūrō went out, fearful that the fence and trees might have fallen. But the fence made of cypress wood stood where it always had. Lying underneath it, however, Kojūrō saw something he'd been seeing all his life, something dark reddish. His heart almost stopped. Lately he had been thinking with some concern about the bear. He went closer. It was indeed the same bear, dead, its head lying in a sea of blood which had poured out of its mouth.

Kojūrō clasped his hands and prayed.

One January morning, as he was getting ready to go out, Kojūrō said to his mother something he had never before said:

"Granny, I've gotten old. This morning, for the first time since I was born, I don't feel like getting in the water."

His ninety-year-old mother, who was spinning on the sunny side of the veranda, raised her almost blind eyes toward him for a moment and made an expression which seemed to be both smiling and crying. Kojūrō finished tying his straw sandals, rose to his feet with a groan, and walked out. The children, who were in the stable, stuck their heads out one by one.

"Grandpa, come home soon," they called, laughing.

Kojūrō looked up at the blue polished sky before turning to his grandchildren to say, "Now I'm going." Then he started up the dazzling hard snow toward the White Valley.

The dog was soon panting, sticking its red tongue out, as it ran on and stopped, ran on and stopped. When Kojūrō disappeared behind the hill, the children began to play a game with millet straws.

In the White Valley, Kojūrō walked upstream along the shore. The stream was sky-blue where it made pools, and where it was frozen, it looked like glass panes laid out. In some places, countless icicles hung like rosaries. Occasionally, red and yellow spindle fruit peeked like flowers out of the bushes on the banks. Kojūrō saw the two shadows, his own and the dog's, glisten as they moved along. The shadows were a crisp indigo like the ones the birches cast on the snow.

During the past summer, he had made sure that just beyond the mountain over the White Valley there lived a large bear.

After crossing five streams coming into the valley and wading from right to left, left to right, he reached a small waterfall. Immediately from its bottom, he began to climb the cliff toward the Long Range. The snow was so dazzling it seemed aflame, and he felt as if he were wearing purple eyeglasses.

His dog followed him well up the cliff, sometimes slipping, sometimes hugging the snow. The cliff-top was a mildly sloping flat land with chestnut trees growing sparsely. In the wind, the snow glared like crystalline limestone. The surrounding mountain peaks were all snowcapped.

It happened when Kojūrō was taking a rest on the cliff-top. Suddenly, the dog started to bark as if set afire. Kojūrō turned back and saw the large bear he had marked during the summer charging toward him on its hind legs.

Calmly he held his gun ready, his legs planted in the snow. But the charging bear didn't slow down, its loglike arms limply raised, running straight on. Kojūrō turned a little pale.

Cruck! Kojūrō heard his gun explode. But the bear pressed forward, a swaying black storm. The dog bit the bear's leg. The next instant, Kojūrō's head clanged, and all at once everything turned blue. Then he heard these words in the distance:

"Oh, Kojūrō, I didn't mean to kill you."

"I'm dead," Kojūrō thought. Then he saw dots of light like blue stars twinkle, twinkle all around. "This is how you know your death. That's the fire you see when you die." Then he said in his head, "Bears, forgive me."

What he might have felt after that, I don't know.

Three days later, at night, there was a moon like an ice ball hanging in the sky. The snow shone pale blue, and the water burned phosphorescent. The Pleiades and Orion twinkled green and olive, as if breathing.

On the flat cliff-top with chestnut trees, surrounded by snowcapped mountain peaks, a number of large black creatures had gathered in a circle, each casting a black shadow. Their upper bodies bent forward on the snow, like praying Moslems, they did not move for a long, long time. In the light of the snow and the moon, you could see, placed on the highest spot, Kojūrō's dead body, half sitting.

Maybe it was our imagination, but his dead frozen face was as clear as when he was alive, a half smile lingering on it. The three stars of Orion reached mid-heaven and then moved westward, but the large black creatures did not move, as if turned to stone.

The texts of the poems and stories translated here are based mainly on the twelve-volume "complete works" of Miyazawa Kenji, published by Chikuma Shōbō between 1967 and 1969. The later "complete works," in fifteen volumes, published by the same house between 1973 and 1978, was also consulted. Words and phrases given in a foreign language in the original texts are usually italicized in the translations.

The poems in this book are presented in chronological order except for the piece "Proem," which is placed where it is because Miyazawa wrote it as an introduction to his first collection of poems and placed it at the beginning of the book.

———

Spring & Asura: For Asura, see the Introduction. The repeated line "I am Asura incarnate" is an inexact, even incorrect, translation of the original, *Ore wa hitori no shura na no da* (more faithfully, "I am an asura"), on two counts. The Japanese word *ashura* (*asura* in Sanskrit) means the king as well as the ordinary denizens of the Asura Realm; here Miyazawa says he is one of the lesser ones. Also, the use of "incarnate" contradicts Buddhist belief, which takes for granted the continuing existence of the Asura Realm, along with the five other realms. My translation, however, is an attempt to retain the assertive tone of the original line. As in "Voiceless Grief," *ashura* also means the Asura Realm.

Zypressen (German) means "cypresses." T'ien-shan ("Heaven's Mountain") is a mountain range west of China where important trade routes ran to central Asia. Buddhists venerate it because their religion came through the region. "True Words" refers to the Shingon ("True Word") sect of Buddhism.

Daybreak: The last phrase is from the *Prajnaparamita Hrdaya Sutra* (popularly known as the *Heart Sutra*), which may be translated: "Those who have gone to the other side, enlightenment, be happy."

Annelid Dancer: In the original, the title is given both in German, *Annelide Tanzerin*, and in Japanese, *Zenchū maite.* Since the poem apparently describes mosquito larvae, the term *annelide* is incorrect. *Zenchū*, rendered here as "wormy worm," may be Miyazawa's pseudo-scientific coinage; *zen* means "moving like a soft worm," and *chū*, "worm," "insect."

"The hard keyura *jewels . . .":* Keyura (Sanskrit) is jewelry worn by Indian nobles and used to decorate Buddhist images and temples.

Koiwai Farm: The last "part" of this sequence, evidently written in a single day, is numbered 9, but Miyazawa appears not to have written Part 8, and he excluded Parts 5 and 6 when he included the sequence in his only published book of poems, *Spring & Asura*. After the publication of the book, he marked those lines he wanted deleted in a future edition. In this translation Parts 5 and 6 are restored, and some—though not all—of the lines marked for deletion are retained.
 ~~Der Freischütz~~ (German) means "the marksman" and is a casual reference to Weber's opera with that title.
 Der heilige Punkt (German) means "the holy spot." *Larix* (German) means "larch."

The Landscape Inspector: The Purkinje effect is a perceptual discovery made by J. E. Purkinje (1787–1869).

Haratai Sword-Dancing Troupe: The poem describes a local festival dance. Akuroō ("King Evil Path") was the legendary leader of the people who inhabited the northern region of Japan before they were conquered and driven out by the emperor's commander-in-chief Sakanoue no Tamuramaro (758–811) in 801. Legend has it that the king and his people lived in the cave called Takoku.

Massaniello: T. A. Massaniello (1620–1647) was a Naples fisherman turned revolutionary. *Haori:* A type of kimono worn like a jacket.

The Last Farewell: This and the three poems that follow were written for Toshiko (1898–1922), Kenji's sister. Tushita Heaven is the region presided over by the Bodhisattva Maitreya.

White Birds: Prince Yamato Takeru is a military hero in the *Kojiki* (Record of Ancient Matters), a semimythological account of Japanese history compiled in 712.

Okhotsk Elegy: Saghalien is an island in the Sea of Okhotsk, north of Hokkaido, Japan. When the island was divided between Russia and Japan in 1905, the southern half became known as Karafuto. Eihama, now called Starodubskoe, was a port town in Karafuto.

Namo Saddharmapundarika Sutra (Sanskrit) is a Buddhist recitation, which may be translated: "I revere the Sutra of the Lotus of the Wonderful Law."

Commandments Forbidding Greed & Desire: Jiun (1718–1804) is a renowned monk of the Shingon Sect of Buddhism.

Winter and Galaxy Station: Josef Pasternack (1881–1940) was a Polish-born American orchestral conductor.

Rest: Eccolo qua (Italian) means "He's here" or "It's here."

Reservoir Note: Mr. Shirafuji is Shirafuji Rinnosuke, Miyazawa's colleague at the agricultural school and a leading disciple of the Buddhist scholar and preacher Shimaji Taitō. Meeting Shimaji and reading his Japanese translation of the *Lotus Sutra*, Miyazawa became a devout follower of the Shingon Sect.

Spring: Bonan Tagon, Shinjoro (Esperanto) means "Good afternoon, how are you?"

An Opinion Concerning a Proposed National Park Site: Yama is the Judge of the Buddhist underworld.

Mr. Pamirs the Scholar Takes a Walk: Hsi-yu is the old Chinese name for the region of Central Asia. Nagarjuna (c. A.D. 100–200) is a great Buddhist preacher and philosopher. Kucha is one of the thirty-six countries of Hsi-yu.

Spring ("The air melts"): CZ was one of the classifications for the Japanese railroad trains in Miyazawa's day.

Cabbage Patch: Suiko was an empress (554–628) during whose reign Japanese culture reached its earlier zenith. The great Hōryū-ji temple was built while she was ruler. Iyasaka-ism is the form of "Japanism" advocated by the then-governor of Iwate, which required its followers to shout *Iyasaka* ("Greater Prosperity") instead of the traditional *Banzai* ("Long Live the Emperor").

253

The Master of the Field: Juryōbon ("Duration of Life") is Chapter 15 of the *Lotus Sutra*, which deals with the inestimable age of the Lord Buddha.

The Prefectural Engineer's Statement Regarding Clouds: For *Kojiki*, see the note to "White Birds."

A Rice-Growing Episode: Riku-u No. 132 is a species of rice developed to withstand cold weather. In Miyazawa's time, it was officially recommended, but now other, newly developed species are preferred.

Untitled (1090): Myōga is a variety of ginger cultivated for the edible shoots.

October 20th: Mahābrahmadevaloka (Sanskrit) means "Great Father, the World Honored One" and, as an invocation, may be comparable to "Jesus Christ, Our Lord."

Hiroaki Sato has published a dozen books of Japanese poems in English translation. Among them, *From the Country of Eight Islands*, an anthology of Japanese poetry on which he collaborated with Burton Watson, won the American P.E.N. translation prize for 1982. He is also the author of *The Sword and the Mind*, a translation of seventeenth-century treatises on swordsmanship and Zen; *That First Time*, a book of poems; and a book, in Japanese, about haiku composed in English. A resident of New York since 1968, he writes a biweekly column, "Here and Now—in New York," for the *Mainichi Daily News* and reviews books for the *New York Times Book Review* and other periodicals.

Design by David Bullen
Typeset in Mergenthaler Granjon
by Wilsted & Taylor
Printed by Haddon Craftsmen
on acid-free paper